# ON FOOT IN JOSHUA TREE

## A Comprehensive Hiking Guide to a National Park Service Area

Patty A. Furbush

M.I. Adventure Publications

First printing, March 1986
Second edition, March 1987
Third edition, February 1992

Manufactured in the United States of America

ISBN 0-9616395-3-9

Library of Congress Catalog Card Number: 91-66372

M.I. Adventure Publications
RFD#1 472
West Lebanon, Maine 04027

*To my parents*

Lt. Col. and Mrs. Richard D. Furbush


## Acknowledgments

Special Thanks to Kip Knapp, Jim Schlinkmann, Colette Bien, and Dan Wirth for accompanying me on many of my hikes; to Jim Schlinkmann, Peggy Furbush, Lois and Robert Diefendorf, Aleta McCardle, Mary Nutter, Colette Bien, and Terry Lee for assiting with the technical preparation of this book; and to Gary Garrett, Bill Truesdell, Joan Jackson, Kip Knapp, and Pat Flanagan for providing assistance with my research.

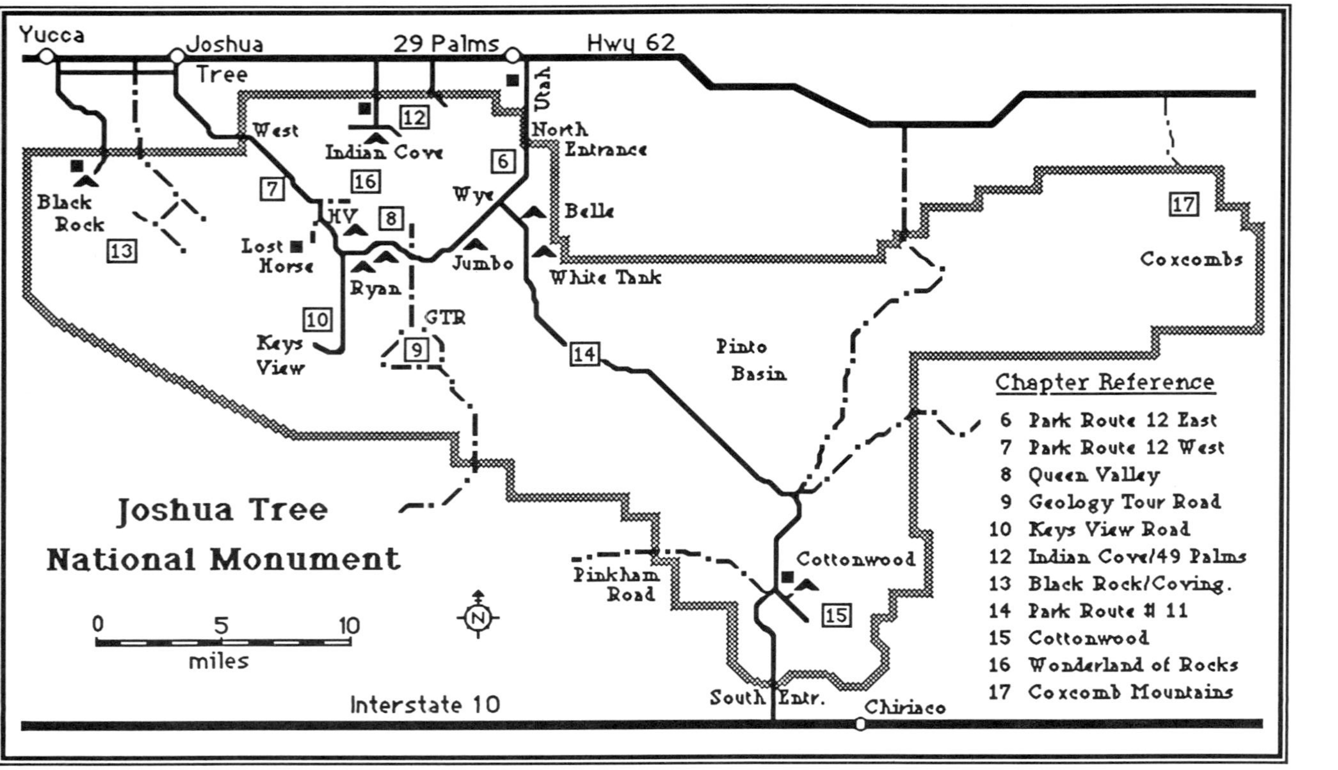
Yucca
Joshua Tree
29 Palms
Hwy 62
Utah
North Entrance
West
Indian Cove
12
6
7
16
Wye
Belle
Black Rock
13
HV
8
Lost Horse
Ryan
Jumbo
White Tank
10
GTR
9
Keys View
14
Pinto Basin
17
Coxcombs
Chapter Reference
6 Park Route 12 East
7 Park Route 12 West
8 Queen Valley
9 Geology Tour Road
10 Keys View Road
12 Indian Cove/49 Palms
13 Black Rock/Coving.
14 Park Route # 11
15 Cottonwood
16 Wonderland of Rocks
17 Coxcomb Mountains
Joshua Tree
National Monument
Pinkham Road
Cottonwood
15
0 5 10
miles
Interstate 10
South Entr.
Chiriaco

# Table of Contents

## Area Maps



## Topographical Maps

## **Author's Note:** Monument or Park

---

As this book goes to press, it is uncertain whether Joshua Tree will remain a national monument or become a national park. A bill has been introduced before Congress which could change Joshua Tree National Monument to Joshua Tree National Park. The bill has passed through the House of Representatives and is now in the hands of the Senate.

A change in designation from monument to park will not change the level of protection for the area. The main difference between a national park and a national monument is the means in which the area is established. National monuments are created by presidential proclamation. National parks can only be established by Congress.

If the bill does pass, it will have little effect on the hiking in the area. The main exception would be the result of a possible increase in size to the national monument area. New lands which may be added to the monument area will mean additional hiking opportunities within this protected National Park Service area.

# Chapter 1

# JOSHUA TREE NATIONAL MONUMENT

# A SPECIAL PLACE

The pink illumination of dawn cloaks an extensive array of gigantic boulder piles and monolithic rock formations. Rugged mountains cast shadows across an immense basin that stretches mile after seemingly endless mile. As the shadows recede, the rising sun brings forth the color and life of the daylight hours. Delicate white petals of the tidy-tip flower shimmer in the breeze. An antelope ground squirrel scampers past the flower leaving a repeating pattern in the sand. Overhead a high-pitched cry emits from a solitary red-tailed hawk as he circles in the vivid blue skies. Deep within an isolated canyon, the mysterious descending echoes of a canyon wren ring forth from beneath a sentinel of palm trees.

The warm sun continues its daily journey across the open skies, and eventually the shadows begin to lengthen. As dusk descends, the pink illumination returns to highlight a high rocky cliff from where a golden eagle takes flight. An owl hoots and two coyotes exchange eerie howls in the approaching darkness. Black forests of still and multiarmed tree-figures create a grand silhouette against a sunset blaze of oranges and reds. A sea of stars begins sparkling throughout the clear night skies. The colorless land now cloaked in darkness beckons forth the life of the nighttime hours....

These are the intricate images of the vast and interwoven wonders of a desert wilderness. It is a wilderness that is among one of this country's national treasures. It is a wilderness whose life, secrets and magic cannot be fully enjoyed and appreciated until it is traveled and explored on foot.

Joshua Tree National Monument, located in the heart of southern California, is this wilderness treasure. It is an 870 square mile hikers' playground. The area attracts multitudes of people who drive the roads to gaze upon desert wonders. However, the backcountry remains quiet, undisturbed and offers a beautiful, adventuresome retreat for those willing to set out on foot. The Colorado and Mojave Deserts merge within this desert playground creating an opportunity to compare and explore two separate desert ecosystems.

*Joshua trees frame giant boulders in the Mojave Desert*

## Mojave Desert

The Mojave Desert, which predominates the central and western half of the monument, is the higher, wetter, and cooler of the two desert ecosystems. It exists largely at elevations greater than 2000' and hence is commonly called the high desert. The Mojave is home for the large forests of Joshua trees, which grow only at elevations over 3000'. Joshua trees are not actually trees but are yucca plants, members of the agave family.

A second beautiful curiosity that exists within this higher portion of the monument is the unique collection of gigantic boulder formations that tower above the Joshua trees. The mere sight of this geologic oddity makes one wonder what magnificent force rolled these rocks together to create the formations. The boulder piles were actually formed underground when liquid rock oozed up, cooled, and crystallized beneath the core of existing older rock known as Pinto gneiss. Water filtered down through the Pinto gneiss into the joints of the younger monzogranite rock and transformed the outer layers of this new rock into clay. The clay then eroded away leaving the monzogranite with rounded edges. Uplifting and erosion of the older rock gradually worked to expose the monzogranite boulder formations on the earth's surface.

## Colorado Desert

The Colorado Desert, which predominates the southern and eastern half of the monument, lies at an elevation generally less than 3000'. Although Joshua trees don't grow in this low desert, it has its own characteristic vegetation. Ocotillo and the jumping cholla cactus are among the most notable of the Colorado Desert plants. There are a greater variety and a more abundance of cacti than in the Mojave. There is also a greater variety of trees. Mesquite, palo verdes, and smoke trees flourish along many of the sandy washes.

*A carpet of desert dandelions surrounds an ocotillo*

One feature that cannot go unmentioned when describing the Colorado Desert section of the monument is the Pinto Basin. This immense basin, measuring close to 200 square miles, is mostly untouched by road or human foot. Only two roads travel through the basin. Park Route #11 travels along the southwestern edge of the basin, and Old Dale Road -- a dirt road -- travels north to south through the center of the basin. The majority of the basin remains a wilderness.

## Oases and Mountains

Five oases provide a third type of ecosystem which can be found within the monument. The life that centers around these vibrant islands is a contrast to the arid surroundings in which they are found. Water, either on the surface or not far below, nourishes concentrations of lush grasses, native fan palms, cottonwoods and other water-loving plants. The oases provide an important life source and home for numerous species of plants, birds, and other wildlife.

Mountains are located throughout the monument both in and around the Colorado and Mojave deserts and around the oases. They are the high, rugged, rocky mountains of the Little San Bernardino, Hexie, Pinto, Coxcomb, Eagle and Cottonwood mountain ranges. In the cooler, moister, upper reaches of these mountains is yet a fourth type of habitat. Pinyon pines, junipers, scrub oak, and red-barked manzanita, intermingled with the more commonly associated desert vegetation, provide for beautiful terrain and additional variety for hikers and backpackers.

## Wildlife

On foot in the quiet backcountry is the best way to seek and enjoy the desert wildlife. There are about 40 species of reptiles and amphibians and 40 species of mammals that make their home in the monument. Some of the more notable mammal species include desert bighorn sheep and mountain lions. In addition, over 200 species of birds have been recorded within the monument. The National Audubon Society considers Joshua Tree National Monument one of the best birding areas in Southern California.

Each individual species of wildlife within the monument is an important and inseparable part of the desert ecosystem. The feared rattlesnake and uncomely chuckwalla lizard are as equally important in the desert web of life as the red-tailed hawk, the coyote, and the desert bighorn. Use one of the several pamphlets available from the visitor centers or from the information boxes (scattered throughout the monument) to learn about, identify, and locate the abundance of wildlife.

## History

In the early days before the monument was established, there was another form of wildlife that made its home in this desert area; it was man. Thousands of years ago, some of the southwest's earliest human inhabitants lived in a fertile valley that existed in the Pinto Basin. Pinto Man made his home along a river which flowed through this valley. Arrow points and stone tools found at the homesite of this primitive man serve as pieces to a puzzle of a culture long past.

Millennias after Pinto Man and the river disappeared, Indians used the monument area as a hunting ground and seasonal home. Tokens of their presence -- arrow points, pottery, and petroglyphs -- have been found throughout the monument. Two tribes of Indians, the Serrano and the Chemehuevi, made a permanent home at the Oasis of Mara, part of the present-day monument. When white man arrived, this oasis provided a place of peaceful coexistence for both Indian and pioneer.

Thc latc 1800's brought the first white settlers to the southern California Desert. Cattlemen, miners, and other pioneers made a home and life in and around what is now the monument. Cattlemen grazed their herds on desert grasses and built water-holding tanks. The tanks were constructed by building small dams of rock and cement across the width of a wash. Rain run-off collected behind the walls and provided water for cattle during dry periods. Today these tanks can be found throughout the monument. Although there are still a few that retain water, most of the tanks have since filled with sand.

The discovery of gold brought a different emphasis to the use of the land. Mines, mills, and small mining towns sprang up throughout the desert. Most of the mines within the monument were worked until profits could no longer be gained. Then man moved on leaving the desert to heal its scars.

One man that didn't move on was William F. Keys. Keys arrived about 1910 and soon after began to build his lifetime home within the current boundaries of the monument. He raised a family on the Desert Queen Ranch where he grew crops, grazed cattle, and worked nearby mines and mills. Even after the monument was established, Keys continued to live on his beloved ranch until his death in 1969. Today the ranch can be visited by taking scheduled tours with the Joshua Tree Natural History Association. Except for its slow deterioration back to nature, the ranch remains as Keys left it. It is an authentic testimony to the pioneer way of life.

By the early 1900's, the number of people visiting the California Desert was increasing dramatically. Unfortunately, damage to the desert was increasing even more dramatically. Large amounts of cacti were being removed for transplant into home cactus gardens. Joshua trees were burned by visitors as nighttime street lights.

In the late 1920's, Mrs. Minerva Hoyt recognized these problems and began a crusade to save the desert area which is now Joshua Tree National Monument. Her proposal to protect the area as a park or monument was enthusiastically received by President Franklin Roosevelt. In 1936 a 825,000 acre monument was established. (As a result of mining pressure in 1950, the size of the monument was reduced to its present size of 560,000 acres.) Thanks to the insight of Mrs. Hoyt, Joshua Tree National Monument has been preserved so all may continue to explore and enjoy this desert wilderness.

Some unknowing people consider the desert a wasteland. Perhaps Joshua Tree National Monument may appear a wasteland to those who are not willing to explore the desert's abounding life, its colorful history, and subtle, yet sometimes profound beauty. However, those who are willing to explore and discover the monument will find a special magic and life within the open valleys, secluded canyons, and high mountains. They will know this desert as a treasure to be explored, cherished, and protected. Given time, Joshua Tree National Monument is certain to become a special place that finds its way to the heart.

# Chapter 2

# GENERAL INFORMATION

The following information will be useful as a reference both for new visitors to Joshua Tree National Monument and for returning visitors.

## Weather

Throughout most of the year, the monument has a very favorable climate for hiking. In fact, the weather seems ideal with an average maximum temperature of 82.9°F, average minimum temperature of 51.7°F, average precipitation of 4.17" a year, and an average of 259 clear days per year. However, there are times of the year when conditions are not desirable for hiking. Temperatures in midsummer will often climb over 100° F. During these times, hiking is not advised in the lower, open areas such as Pinto Basin. Thunderstorms and downpours usually occur during July and August. These storms will sometimes precipitate flash floods -- a serious danger of which hikers should be wary.

Winter months may bring occasional accumulations of snow in the higher portions of the monument. Usually the snow completely melts in one or two days. Snow or no snow, backpackers are warned to prepare for radical temperature extremes between night and day. Throughout the winter there may be several days of tee-shirt weather. When the sun sets, however, the temperature quickly drops, and warm jackets and sweaters become a necessity.

The wind can sometimes be quite bothersome, especially during the cooler months of the year. Wind velocities may exceed 25 - 35 mph. This is not necessarily time to give up on hiking, but perhaps it is time to seek a sheltered route.

The following data compiled by the National Park Service will assist in preparing for hikes at different times of the year. These weather readings were taken at Monument Headquarters in Twentynine Palms at an elevation of 1,960 feet. Temperatures at the higher elevations in the monument will average about 10-11° F less. Precipitation at the higher altitudes will average about 3.5" more annually.

| Month | Average Max. °F | Average Min. °F | Average Precipitation | Average Humidity |
|---|---|---|---|---|
| January | 62.0 | 35.1 | .49 | 30.7 |
| February | 67.2 | 38.3 | .31 | 25.0 |
| March | 72.5 | 42.0 | .35 | 21.2 |
| April | 80.7 | 48.9 | .10 | 17.8 |
| May | 89.9 | 56.6 | .07 | 14.6 |
| June | 99.1 | 64.2 | .02 | 13.2 |
| July | 104.7 | 71.5 | .66 | 17.9 |
| August | 102.8 | 70.2 | .73 | 20.0 |
| September | 96.7 | 63.4 | .46 | 17.2 |
| October | 84.5 | 52.7 | .36 | 19.9 |
| November | 71.2 | 41.5 | .31 | 29.9 |
| December | 63.1 | 36.0 | .51 | 35.8 |

## Camping

Seven campgrounds, collectively containing over 400 sites, are available within the monument on a first-come-first-served basis. In addition, there are twenty-two reservable group campsites at Cottonwood, Indian Cove, and Sheep Pass campgrounds and about 100 reservable family sites at Black Rock Campground.

Six of the first-come-first-served campgrounds are free of charge. No water is available in these campgrounds, and the only toilet facilities are outhouses. There are picnic tables and fire grates in all sites. Two campgrounds, Cottonwood and Black Rock, do have water and flush toilets and charge a fee. There are no hookups anywhere in the monument.

Usually all campgrounds will fill on warm weekends starting on Labor Day weekend and continuing through Memorial Day weekend. All campgrounds are subject to seasonal closures. Call the monument visitor center for up-to-date information on closures and availability.

## Facilities

Other than campgrounds and a few picnic areas, there are no facilities within the monument. The towns of Joshua Tree, Twentynine Palms, and Yucca Valley, along the north boundary of the monument, and Chiriaco Summit, along the south boundary of the monument, provide the nearest locations for gas, stores, lodging, and dining.

## Visitor Centers and Ranger Stations

Water, assistance, and information may be obtained at the Oasis Visitor Center, Cottonwood Visitor Center, Indian Cove Ranger Station, and Black Rock Ranger Station. Water is not available at any other location within the monument. Assistance and information are also available at the North and West Entrance Stations. All visitor centers, ranger stations, and entrance stations are subject to seasonal closures. The Oasis Visitor Center in Twentynine Palms is the exception. It is open year round, seven days a week.

## General Regulations

The following regulations should be helpful to those not familiar with National Park Service areas. This is only a partial list containing those rules that are commonly overlooked or misunderstood. Contact a ranger or inquire at a visitor center if there are any questions about regulations.

- No weapons of any kind are allowed within the monument.
- All vegetation, dead or alive, is protected and therefore may not be collected or burned.
- All wildlife (including snakes and scorpions) is protected and therefore may not be killed, harassed, collected, or fed.
- Pets must be kept leashed. They are not allowed in the backcountry.
- Vehicles, including bicycles, are permitted only on established roads.
- Camping is allowed only in designated campgrounds and in the backcountry. (See Chapter 3 for information on backcountry regulations.)
- A permit is required for camping in the backcountry.
- All cultural artifacts are protected. It is prohibited to collect, disturb, or remove any historic or prehistoric artifact.

For additional information, including information on current policies, regulations, and closures, call or write:

Joshua Tree National Monument
74485 National Monument Drive
Twentynine Palms, CA 92277
(619) 367- 7511

# Chapter 3

# HIKING INFORMATION FOR JOSHUA TREE NATIONAL MONUMENT

Hiking in Joshua Tree National Monument is different from hiking in other commonly hiked areas within this country. The information contained in this chapter should be helpful for recognizing and preparing for these differences.

## Route Selection Tips

There are very few trails in Joshua Tree National Monument. Most of the hiking is done along washes, canyons, valleys, ridges, and closed dirt roads. The following tips should be helpful both when following the hike descriptions and when venturing into undescribed areas.

- When there are no roads or trails, it is generally easier to travel in the washes and along ridges rather than through the open desert. Use of these travel aids eliminates time-consuming zigzagging around spotted vegetation.
- Old dirt roads closed to vehicle traffic are another travel aid. However, be advised that many of the dirt roads marked on the earlier topographic maps can no longer be found. Time has erased their mark.
- Distance can be deceiving in the wide open spaces of the desert. What appears to be a short walk away may be hours away and visa versa. Use a topographical map to determine distances.
- Many desert landmarks look similar. Study and take note of your surroundings for the return trip. Keep track of your location on a topographical map.

## Planning & Preparing

The following information is provided to assist with the planning and preparing for both day and overnight hikes.

**Backcountry Registration**: All overnight backcountry users must register before heading into the backcountry. A non-fee permit may be obtained through self-registration at any one of the twelve backcountry boards located throughout the monument. The top half of the permit is carried with the backpacking group, and the bottom half is deposited at the board. A backcountry board parking area is the only place a vehicle may be left overnight. For any exceptions to this rule, permission must be obtained from a ranger.

**Special Equipment**: Following are some equipment needs for desert hiking.

- For overnight and full day trips, clothing is needed for both temperature extremes -- warm days and cold nights.
- A hat, sunglasses and sunscreen are recommended to protect against the bright desert sun.
- For off-trail hikes, long pants are desirable to protect against rough desert brush.
- Good walking shoes or tennis shoes are adequate for the easier hikes. Sturdy, lightweight hiking boots which provide good ankle support are essential for cross-country hikes or hikes in rugged, mountainous terrain.
- A map, compass, and orienteering skills are recommended for all but the most straightforward trail hikes (*i.e.* nature trails).

**Water:** Water in the backcountry can be found in only a few places and only at certain times of the year. Never depend upon finding a natural water source unless first hand information is available. Even then, a natural water source should not be the primary source of water. Before drinking any water from these areas, boil the water for at least ten minutes or use a water purifying pump. During the warm parts of the year, each hiker should plan on carrying at least one gallon of water per day. (Freeze-dried food is not recommended for desert use because of the need for extra water.)

**Fragile Environment -- Rules and Ethics:** The backcountry of the monument bares few scars of overuse or misuse (disregarding mining scars). Most of the people who explore the monument through hiking follow the Minimum Impact Ethic: Hike in and enjoy the monument, but leave it in its natural and undisturbed state so that others that follow may enjoy the same. There are regulations that must be followed; but in addition, every hiker needs to abide by the Minimum Impact Ethic. The following are National Park Service regulations and guidelines that keep within this ethic.

- Trail use and route selection: Hike on trails where they are provided. When hiking through areas that have no trails, attempt to travel in the sandy washes, on rocky ground, or in other unvegetated areas. Unthoughtful route selection by groups can result in destruction of the thin desert-soil crust, trampling of delicate vegetation, erosion, and creation of unnecessary trails. It can take more than a hundred years for the soil and vegetation of the fragile desert to recover from careless human impact.

- Campsite selection: There are no established backcountry campgrounds. Campsite locations are selected at the discretion of each hiking party with the use of a few site selection rules. (This is the current Joshua Tree National Monument policy and is subject to change. Check on existing policies before planning an overnight trip.) Do not camp within one mile of any road nor within 500 feet of any trail. Set up tents in areas having little or no vegetation. (Be aware of the flash flood danger if camp is set up near a wash.) Campsites must be located at least 200 feet from any water source. This will prevent pollution of this limited resource and permit access for wildlife. Do not level sites, dig trenches, or build rock structures. This causes soil disturbance and leaves visible signs of human presence.

- Fires: No open fires are allowed in the backcountry due to the danger of wildfire. Campfires scar and sterilize the soil, and their remains create an eyesore. Self-contained backpacking stoves are recommended.

- Garbage and litter: All garbage and litter must be carried out of the backcountry. Buried refuse is usually dug up by animals and scattered by the wind. Any substance foreign to the desert such as garbage, orange peels, cigarette butts, and paper will take years to decompose in the arid environment. (Do not remove "historical litter," i.e. equipment, cans, etc. that have been left by pioneers and miners.)

- Human waste: Catholes, small holes dug about 6" deep, should be used for disposal of human feces. Cover the holes with soil and make the area look as natural as possible. Catholes should be located at least 200 feet from any water source. Pack out all toilet paper in a plastic bag rather than burying or burning it.

- Water source: Never wash in or near a water source. Conserve water from these natural sources; remember, wildlife depends upon this water for survival.

- Day use areas: Certain areas in the monument are restricted to day use. (Refer to the section "Understanding Day Use Areas...", page 15.) Before backpacking near one of these areas, go to a visitor center and have the restricted area outlined on a topographical map. As an alternative, use the map drawings and topographical maps in this book to assist in identifying the boundaries of the day use areas. (See Chapter 4, Maps and Compass Directions.)

## Hazards - Use Caution

The following are some dangers that hikers might be exposed to while traveling in the monument. Observing the suggested precautions could keep an enjoyable hike from becoming an unpleasant, or even tragic experience.

**Mines and Buildings**: Mines and building ruins provide an interesting historical emphasis to hikes; they also provide a potential hazard. No mine shaft should be considered safe for entry. The shafts are composed mainly of crumbling unsupported rock. The timber shoring that exists in some mines is rotten. Vertical mine shafts are especially dangerous since the ground surrounding the shaft's opening may be undercut and weak. Some of these shafts drop straight down for hundreds of feet. Wooden building structures should also be considered unsafe for entry due to rotting wood. Enjoy and explore the mines and buildings but only on the outside.

**Flash Floods**: Heavy rains, even for short periods, may be accompanied by flash floods in mountain or hilly areas. Flash floods most commonly occur during July and August but may occur during any period of heavy rain. To avoid this danger, keep alert to weather conditions. Don't camp or hike in canyons and washes during rainy periods. Never attempt to cross a flooded wash; the water level is apt to rise quickly and with little warning.

**Snakes and Other Misunderstoods:** The California Desert is home to many varieties of snakes, scorpions, spiders, lizards and insects. Certain species of these creatures do deserve respect and caution, but not the amount of fear they usually instill.

- Snakes: There are six varieties of rattlesnakes within the monument. These snakes are not aggressive. They do provide a danger when they are provoked, surprised or stepped on. Use caution when stepping down off an overhanging rock or when walking through thick bushes. During the hot part of the day, snakes stay in the shade under bushes and rocks. In the cooler evening, they can be found in the open roads or washes. They hibernate during the winter and usually are not found between November and early March. (Note: During numerous years of extensive hiking in the monument, the author encountered only four rattlesnakes while hiking. These four snakes showed no aggressive behavior.)

- Lizards: There are no known poisonous lizards in the monument.

- Scorpions: Although the inflicted sting of a scorpion (native species) may be painful, it is only potentially fatal if the person stung has a severe allergic reaction. Centruroides, the most poisonous of scorpions, is not known to inhabit the monument.

- Spiders: Tarantulas (native species) are commonly active in the spring, summer, and fall months. Even though they are big and look frightening, they cause little harm. They are docile, slow and only mildly poisonous. Rangers frequently pick them up from the roadway with bare hands and remove them to safety. Black Widow Spiders are poisonous and do live in the monument. However, they are not aggressive and their bite is rarely fatal.

A few common sense rules and precautions will help prevent any undesirable encounters with the above creatures. Look carefully before sitting and before placing feet or hands. Keep garbage away from camp areas. Keep campsites clean; food crumbs attract insects and small animals which, in turn, are food for scorpions, spiders, and snakes. Shake out all bedding and clothing before using.

**Vicious Plants**: Certain plants in the monument are responsible for many more inflictions than all the snakes and spiders combined. The thorns of a catsclaw, the pointed unyielding spikes of the yucca, and the barbed spines of the cholla all deserve caution and avoidance when hiking. Unintentional contact with these plants can leave a hiker tending to annoying and painful wounds.

**Weather Related Medical Emergencies**: Due to the temperature extremes at different times of the year, hikers could be faced with the medical emergencies of heat exhaustion, heat stroke, or hypothermia. Be aware of these potential problems, know their signs and symptoms, and know how to treat them.

## Understanding Day Use Areas And Desert Bighorn Sheep

The desert bighorn, a rare subspecies of bighorn sheep, survive in small numbers in isolated places throughout the southwest. Joshua Tree National Monument supports a small population of these animals. The bighorn's prime habitat within the monument is located within the day use areas. It is in these areas that the sheep can find the rugged terrain, isolation, and water pockets that are essential for their survival.

The bighorn residing in Joshua Tree are very shy and nervous animals. Disturbances to their living patterns will cause them to become physically run-down. Under stress, they cease to reproduce. For these reasons it is most important that all human visitation in day use areas be kept to solely daylight hours. This will allow the sheep to roam undisturbed at night and make their way to water sources.

Camping in a day use area or by a water hole will not enhance the chances of seeing a bighorn. It will only keep the sheep away from the area and the water on which they depend. In turn the sheep may weaken and with continued disturbance may die. **Please do not contribute to the decline of the desert bighorn sheep; camp outside of day use areas.**

# Chapter 4

# USING THIS GUIDE

The hikes described in this book are divided into chapters covering twelve different areas within the monument. This will aid in choosing day hikes located near a frontcountry campground basecamp. Information contained in this chapter and in the appendixes at the back of the book will help clarify the individual hike descriptions.

Each hike description is preceded by a reference list of pertinent data. To interpret this data accurately, refer to the section in this chapter entitled "Guide Description Explanations." In all hike descriptions, references will be made to landmarks and starting and ending points. For descriptions and directions to these points, refer to Appendix A, "Landmark Descriptions and Directions."

Hike, explore, and enjoy Joshua Tree National Monument!

## Maps and Compass Directions

Map drawings which show the relationship of hikes to roads, campgrounds, and backcountry boards are provided for each hiking area. The drawings are helpful for choosing and preparing for a hike; however, they should not be used as a substitution for a topographical map. The following map key applies to all the map drawings.

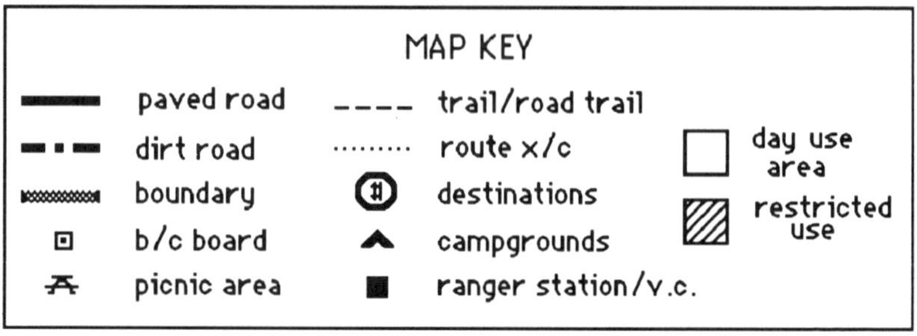

MAP KEY

paved road
dirt road
boundary
b/c board
picnic area
trail/road trail
route x/c
destinations
campgrounds
ranger station/v.c.
day use area
restricted use

Day use areas on these drawings are indicated by thin lines and squares. These squares correspond to numbered section squares (outlined in red) on USGS topographical maps. They may be used to help transpose the day use areas onto USGS maps.

The Wonderland Day Use Area follows geographical features and not section lines. Because of the irregular boundaries, it is difficult to plot this particular day use area on the line maps in this book. The following description may prove helpful: Start at the north boundary of the monument, one mile west of the Indian Cove Road. The day use boundary leads south along the Boy Scout Trail to Keys West Gate. Follow the roads from Keys West Gate, to Echo T, and on to O'Dell Parking Area. Continue east along the south base of Queen Mountain, over to Pine City, then down the canyon past Pine Springs to the North Entrance. From the North Entrance, follow the monument boundary north to Base Line Road then west back to the start. If there is any question about what areas are included in a day use area, inquire at a ranger station or visitor center.

In Appendix D, there is a selection of 15' topographical maps which cover many of the hikes in this book. (Day use areas are marked on these Appendix D maps.) More detailed 7.5' topographical maps may be obtained at the Oasis, Black Rock and Cottonwood visitor centers. The most detailed USGS maps that are available are listed in the information preceding each hike. Another useful map that can be purchased at the information centers is the *Trails Illustrated Topo Map*. This smaller scale topographical map covers the entire monument and has many of the hikes outlined on the map.

In this guide, all compass headings written in the form of numbers or letters (*i.e.* 25°, NW) are field bearings or magnetic north readings. Written directions (*i.e.* north) refer to general true north directions.

## Mileposts

In several of the hike descriptions, reference is made to mileposts. The posts, which are brown with reflective white numbers, are located every two miles along Park Route #11 and Park Route #12. Numbering starts at Pinto Wye for Park Route #11 and at the North Entrance for Park Route #12.

## Guide Description Explanations

The following explains the terms used in the list of pertinent facts that precedes each hike.

Type: Each route is described by one of the following terms:

- trails -- foot trails that are maintained by the National Park Service
- road-trail -- dirt roads that were created before the monument was established. They are closed to vehicle traffic but still provide a route of travel for the hiker.
- cross-country (x/country) -- a hike that uses no man-made travel aids. It may consist of a combination of hiking in washes, along ridges, or through open desert.

Recommendations are also made for conducting the hike as a day or an overnight trip. A hike is not recommended for an overnight trip if the destination lies within a day use area or if there is not a nearby back-country board.

Mileage: All mileages are round trip unless otherwise noted.

Time: All time estimates are based upon the time it takes an average hiker to leisurely complete the trip.

Difficulty: This addresses the strenuousness (first four terms) and technical difficulty (last three terms) of the terrain. Distance is not considered. All hikes are given a rating for strenuousness, while only some are given a rating for difficulty. Hikes with no difficulty rating should be assumed to have little difficulty.

- easy -- generally level or gentle downhill terrain
- moderate -- involves a limited amount of uphill and downhill travel
- moderately strenuous -- involves quite a bit of uphill and downhill travel; terrain provides easier walking than strenuous hikes
- strenuous -- mostly uphill and downhill travel with rocky footing
- moderately difficult -- involves rocky places where some boulder hopping and scrambling is necessary
- difficult -- involves many rocky areas and difficult boulder hopping and scrambling
- difficult (+) -- involves extreme boulder scrambling or areas where some technical rock climbing ability is recommended

Elevation Extremes: lowest and highest points over which a trail or route travels

Starting and Ending Points: Within the monument there are very few directional signs relating to the backcountry. Use Appendix A, "Landmark Descriptions and Directions" to obtain specific directions on how to reach the listed starting and ending points for each hike.

Topographic Diagrams: For most of the hikes in this book, it is easy to judge the strenuousness and character of the hike by taking note of the elevation extremes and differences. However, some of the hikes involve repeated up and down traveling which makes the stated elevation difference somewhat meaningless. Topographic diagrams, such as the one below, are provided for these particular hikes. The diagrams reflect the total elevation gained and lost throughout the hike.

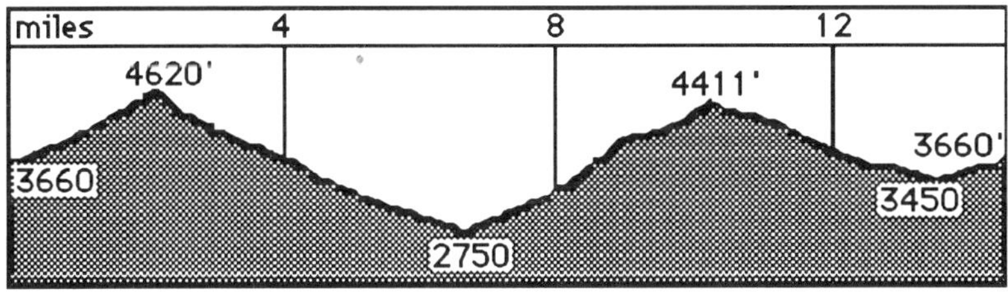

# Chapter 5

## NATURE TRAILS

Throughout the monument there are several short trails ranging from 0.25 to 1.7 miles in length. These trails travel along gentle terrain and lead to some of the highlights of the monument. Along each trail there are interpretive signs which point out the important natural and historical aspects of the area.

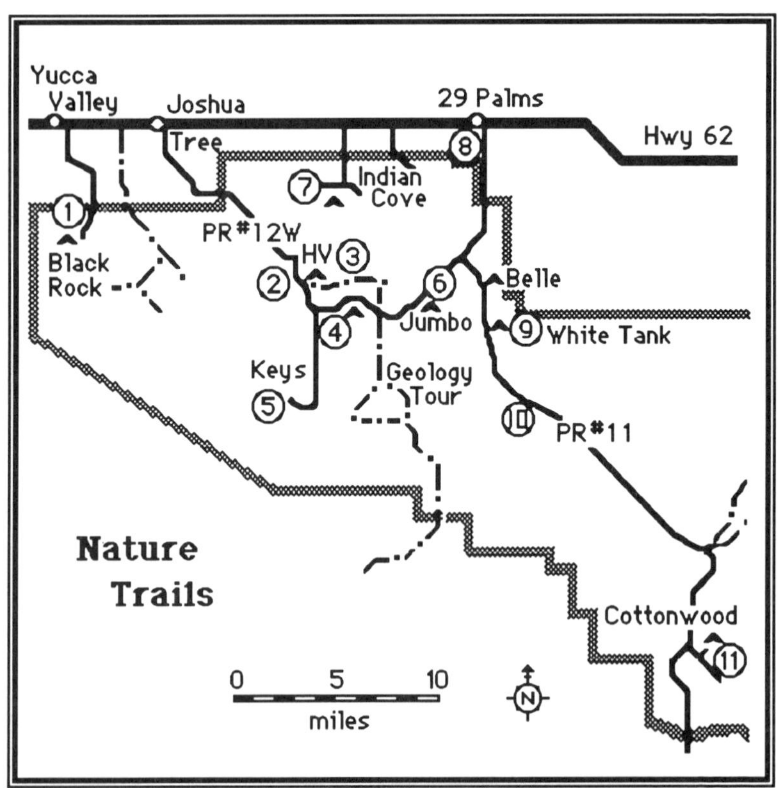

## 1. HIGH VIEW

**Mileage**: 1.3 mile loop
**Starting Point:** South Park Parking Area /Black Rock
**Summary**: This well-maintained, moderately steep (300' elevation gain) trail leads to a good viewpoint of the town of Yucca Valley and Mt. San Gorgonio, an 11,499' peak located in the San Bernardino Mountains. Mt. San Gorgonio, with its winter mantle of snow, provides a beautiful contrast to the desert mountains which surround High View. A trail register is located at the high point on the trail.

Numbered posts line the trail. The corresponding interpretive handout can be obtained at the Black Rock Ranger Station. The handout provides interesting information on plant adaptations to a high desert environment and information on animal relationships with these plants.

The nature trail can also be accessed from the Black Rock Campground. A spur trail, which begins directly west of the ranger station, travels 1/2 mile along thc basc of thc hills and intersects the nature trail just above interpretive stop #2. (Another trail, the South Park Peak trail, Chapter 13, Hike # 2, also begins from the South Park Parking Area.)

*The Hidden Valley Trail winds through boulders*

## 2. HIDDEN VALLEY

**Mileage**: 1 mile loop
**Starting Point:** Hidden Valley Picnic Area
**Summary**: Legend suggests that this rock-enclosed valley was once a hideout for cattle and horse rustlers in the late 1800's. Rocky walls and massive boulder piles create a natural corral that could have contained the stolen cattle and horses. The only easy entrance into the valley is gained through a narrow gap in the rocks.

The trail leaves the parking lot, passes through the narrow gap, and circles around the perimeter of the valley. Joshua Trees, those tall, spiny, tree forms that are characteristic of the Mojave Desert, are scattered throughout the valley. Signs along the trail interpret the history of the area, from the days of prehistoric Indians to the days of cattlemen, ranchers, and miners.

Today the valley is known as a popular area for sport climbing. Watch for rock climbers on the many rock formations located around the valley. (Some easy boulder scrambling will be encountered along the trail.)

## 3. BARKER DAM

**Mileage**: 1 mile loop
**Starting Point**: Barker Dam Parking Area
**Summary**: This hike is located in one of the few easily-accessible areas of the Wonderland. Barker Dam was originally built by cowboys to collect water for cattle. Later, an additional six vertical feet were added to the dam by Pioneer Bill Keys. Keys renamed the dam "Bighorn Dam" and etched this new name into the top of the dam. Today the dam retains a small, beautiful lake framed by the rugged boulders of the Wonderland.

The trail leads past the lake and dam then loops around through Piano Valley before returning to the parking lot. Signs along the way interpret the plant and animal life surrounding a desert water source. The hike involves a short section of easy scrambling between the top and bottom of the dam.

The unusual watering trough below the dam was also built by Keys. It was designed to conserve water, a precious desert resource. The notches on the inner wall of the trough allowed water, sloshed around by drinking cattle, to flow back into the center of the trough rather than out onto the ground.

Follow the trail from the dam through the rock-enclosed Piano Valley. Take a left at the first fork. Travel a few hundred yards to a second trail junction. Continue 100 feet past this junction to view the Disney Petroglyphs located in an elevated rock overhang.

Petroglyphs are carvings made on the rocks by ancient Indians. Experts who study petroglyphs are still uncertain as to whether the carvings were a form of writing or just doodlings. Some of the Disney Petroglyphs are authentic petroglyphs which were unfortunately painted over by a film crew in an attempt to make the carvings more visible. A few of the carvings located on the base the overhang remain undamaged.

Return to the trail junction and turn right (east). Look for the Indian campsite below the cliffs along the right side of the trail. The site can be located by travelling about 100 yards east up the trail from the Disney Petroglyph junction. Look for a tall, lone pine tree growing against the cliff; there is a rock overhang about 40' beyond the tree.

Under the rock overhang, the Indians found shelter and built their campfires. Note the fire-scarred dirt and rock. To the left of the overhang, there are two petroglyphs of ladies. These are believed to be Indian representations of some of the first women pioneers to venture west to this area. Below and about ten feet to the left of the petroglyphs, there is a bedrock mortar, a hole in the rock in which prehistoric Indians ground seed. Return to the trail and continue east back to the parking lot.

## 4. CAP ROCK

**Mileage**: 0.4 mile loop
**Starting Point**: Cap Rock Parking Area
**Summary:** A natural curiosity that exists within this portion of the monument is the unique collection of gigantic boulder piles. The Cap Rock Formation is one of these unusual piles of stone. A large rock perched like a cap on top of a massive pile of boulders prompted the naming of this rock formation.

A level, paved trail leaves Cap Rock and circles through smaller boulder formations. Signs along the trail interpret the geology and plants of the Mojave Desert. (This trail is accessible by wheelchair.)

## 5. KEYS VIEW LOOP

**Mileage:** 0.25 mile loop
**Starting Point:** Keys View
**Summary**: Keys View, which sits on the crest of the Little San Bernardino Mountains, is the highest point in the monument that can be reached by paved road. The area is well known for its spectacular view of the Coachella Valley, Mt. San Jacinto, Mt. San Gorgonio, and the Salton Sea. A paved trail leads to a high viewpoint where hollow tubes direct the human eye to these and several other points of interest -- the Santa Rosa Mts., Indio, Palm Springs, the San Andreas Fault, and Signal Mt. in Mexico (90 miles to the south).

*Skull Rock*

## 6. SKULL ROCK

**Mileage:** 1.7 mile loop
**Starting Point:** Jumbo Rocks Campground or Skull Rock
**Summary**: This trail meanders through boulders, desert washes, and a rocky alleyway. Interpretive signs along the way identify plants and discuss the geology of the Mojave Desert, plant and animal relationships, and plant uses by prehistoric Indians. The trail leads to Skull Rock, an unusual rock formation that can be viewed from the trail as well as from the road. The large monzogranite boulder is shaped in likeness to a gigantic human skull.

The trail can be accessed from three locations: the entrance to Jumbo Rocks Campground; near the entrance to Loop E in the campground; and at Skull Rock, a pull out located a short ways east of the campground on Park Route #12. The trail travels 0.5 miles from Loop E to Skull Rock, crosses the road, and continues 0.7 miles on the other side of Park Route #12 back to the campground entrance. Travel another 1/2 mile along the campground road back to Loop E. The trail is designed to be traveled in a counter clockwise direction.

## 7. INDIAN COVE

**Mileage:** 0.6 mile loop
**Starting Point:** Indian Cove Campground, west end
**Summary:** Indian Cove is nestled in among large monzogranite boulder piles on the northern edge of the Wonderland of Rocks. The Nature Trail skirts around the edge of the boulders and travels through low hills and down a wide sandy wash. Signs along the way interpret the plants and animals of the Mojave Desert, discuss plant and animal relationships, and touch on early Indian life in the area.

While traveling the trail, look for signs of bighorn sheep. Although the sheep are elusive, they are occasionally seen traveling on the rugged formations within the Wonderland. Watch for their silhouette upon a rocky peak.

The nature trail can also be accessed from the group campground between sites 12 and 13. From the group sites, this spur trail travels 1/8 mile and joins the main trail at the most northern section of the loop.

## 8. OASIS OF MARA (Twentynine Palms Oasis)

**Mileage**: 0.5 mile loop
**Starting Point**: Oasis Visitor Center
**Summary**: The Oasis of Mara has been a center of life throughout the history of man's presence in the Southern California Desert. The oasis was initially inhabited by two tribes of Indians, the Serrano and the Chemehuevi, and later by prospectors and homesteaders. When the white man arrived, this oasis provided a place of peaceful coexistence for both Indian and pioneer. Today the only reminder of man's historical presence at this oasis is the gravestone of a young woman who died at the oasis in 1903.

A paved loop trail circles beneath the rustling palms. Signs along the trail identify the plants and interpret the history of the area. A pamphlet, obtained at the start of the trail, provides additional historical information and interprets the natural life of this miniature ecosystem. (This trail is accessible by wheelchair.)

## 9. ARCH ROCK

**Mileage**: 0.3 miles
**Starting Point**: White Tank Campground, opposite Site 9
**Summary**: Signs along this trail interpret the geology of the area and the natural creation of an arch. It took the forces of nature many years to create Arch Rock out of a monzogranite boulder pile. The arch spans a 25' distance and rises about 15' above the underlying boulder. The trail travels past the arch, makes a loop, and exists at Site #12, at the end of the campground.

A short side trip through narrow alleys formed by rock monoliths leads to White Tank. In the early 1900's, cattlemen constructed this tank by building a small dam of rock and cement across the width of the wash. Rain run-off collected behind the wall and provided water for cattle during dry periods. Like most of the many other tanks in the monument, White Tank has since filled with sand. However, it still provides a moist, verdant area attractive to birds and wildlife. The wash above the tank is filled with large boulders and crawl ways which create a playground for children and adults.

To reach White Tank, leave the trail at the Arch Exhibit and travel past the front of the arch. Continue about 100 yards and scramble down through some small boulders.

## 10. CHOLLA CACTUS GARDEN

**Mileage:** 0.25 mile loop
**Starting Point**: Park Route #11, near mile 10
**Summary**: Cholla Cactus Garden is located on the lower edge of the transition zone between the Mojave and Colorado deserts. The Joshua trees of the Mojave Desert do not extend to this lower elevation. They have been replaced by an abundance of creosote, the predominate plant in the Colorado Desert. Cholla Cactus Garden provides a place to examine and learn about the plant and animal life in the Colorado Desert.

The trail travels through an unusually dense concentration of Bigelow cholla, a plant characteristic to both the Mojave and the Colorado deserts. From a distance, the Bigelow cholla looks soft and fuzzy and hence has gained the name teddy bear cholla. However, a close look at the cholla on a hike through the garden will reveal the true identity of the Bigelow. Each plant is covered with fine bristles, and each bristle has a microscopic barb on the exposed end. Even brushing lightly against a cholla can cause the spines to penetrate and stick to skin and clothing. A self-guiding trail guide is available at the start of the trail.

## 11. COTTONWOOD

**Mileage:** 1 mile
**Starting Point:** Cottonwood Campground, sites 13A & 13B
**Summary:** The Cottonwood Nature Trail provides an opportunity to explore and learn about the Colorado Desert. The trail passes through the rolling hills of the Colorado Desert as it travels from the campground to Cottonwood Springs Oasis. Signs along the trail interpret the plants and animals of this desert.

A half mile up the trail, there is a junction in a major wash. The nature trail leads to the right. Traveling to the left leads to the Winona Mill Site (Chapter 15, Hike # 6). The nature trail ends at Cottonwood Spring.

Cottonwood Spring is a significant water source, sometimes producing up to 30 gallons an hour. The thick collection of palm trees and cottonwoods provides important habitat for wildlife in the area. The spring also proved to be an important water source for man during the years of 1870-1910. It was one of the few water sources located along the popular route of travel between Mecca and the Dale Mining District. Pick up the monument brochure entitled "A Day at Cottonwood Spring" to learn more about the area.

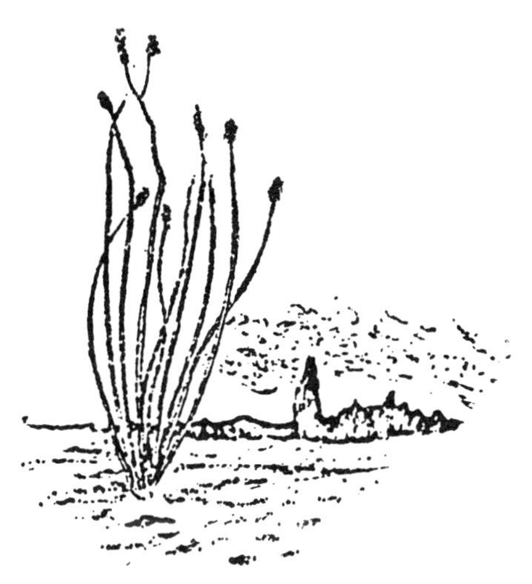

# Chapter 6

# PARK ROUTE #12 EAST

The eastern half of Park Route #12 travels from the monument headquarters and visitor center in Twentynine Palms to Sheep Pass in the center of the monument. The road travels up a large alluvial fan, passes among rugged monzogranite boulders, and continues through Queen Valley to Sheep Pass. Several short, pleasant hikes, as well as longer and more difficult hikes, originate from this road. The North Entrance Backcountry Board is located 0.5 miles inside the entrance. Nearby campgrounds include Jumbo Rocks, located 12 miles from headquarters and four miles east of Sheep Pass, and Belle and White Tank, located a few miles south on Park Route #11. (See map on page 30.)

## 1. OASIS OF MARA - (See Chapter 5, Hike # 8.)

## 2. JOSHUA MOUNTAIN (Indian Head) (3746')

**Type**: x-country, day
**Mileage**: 2.6 miles
**Time**: 2 - 3 hours
**Difficulty**: strenuous, difficult
**Elevation Extremes**: 2570' - 3746' **Difference:** 1176'
**Starting and Ending Point**: Utah Trail, 2.5 miles S of Visitor Center (2570')
**Topo Maps**: Queen Mtn. 7.5'

Summary: Joshua Mountain is an impressive-looking peak with sheer 160' cliffs on the summit block. The shape of the summit block has prompted the nickname of Indian Head. The hike is short but difficult due to the steep, rocky terrain. From the summit there is a panoramic view of Twentynine Palms, the surrounding desert mountains, and the large alluvial fan that descends from the monument.

Route: From the roadside parking on Utah Trail, the peak can be seen to the west. Hike up the obvious steep gully which leads to the south base of Indian Head. Go around to the north side by traveling to either side of the summit block. Scramble up to the summit via the steep north-facing slope. (See Map # 2, Appendix D.)

*Mojave Yucca in bloom at the base of Joshua Mountain*

## 3. CONTACT MINE

**Type**: road-trail / x-country, day
**Mileage**: 3.4 miles
**Time**: 2 - 3 hours
**Difficulty**: moderately strenuous
**Elevation Extremes**: 2920'- 3640' **Difference:** 720'
**Starting and Ending Point**: North Entrance Exhibit (2920')
**Topo Maps**: Queen Mtn. 7.5'

Summary: The Contact Mine is not historically significant but may prove noteworthy to those who have an interest in the early mining era. Building ruins, machinery, tram tracks, a cable winch (pictured on page 31), and a few partially collapsed shafts remain at this once successful mining area. The mine reportedly realized substantial profits in gold and silver in the early 1900's. (The mine shafts are dangerous; maintain a safe distance from the openings. Refer to Chapter 3, "Hazards -- Use Caution.")

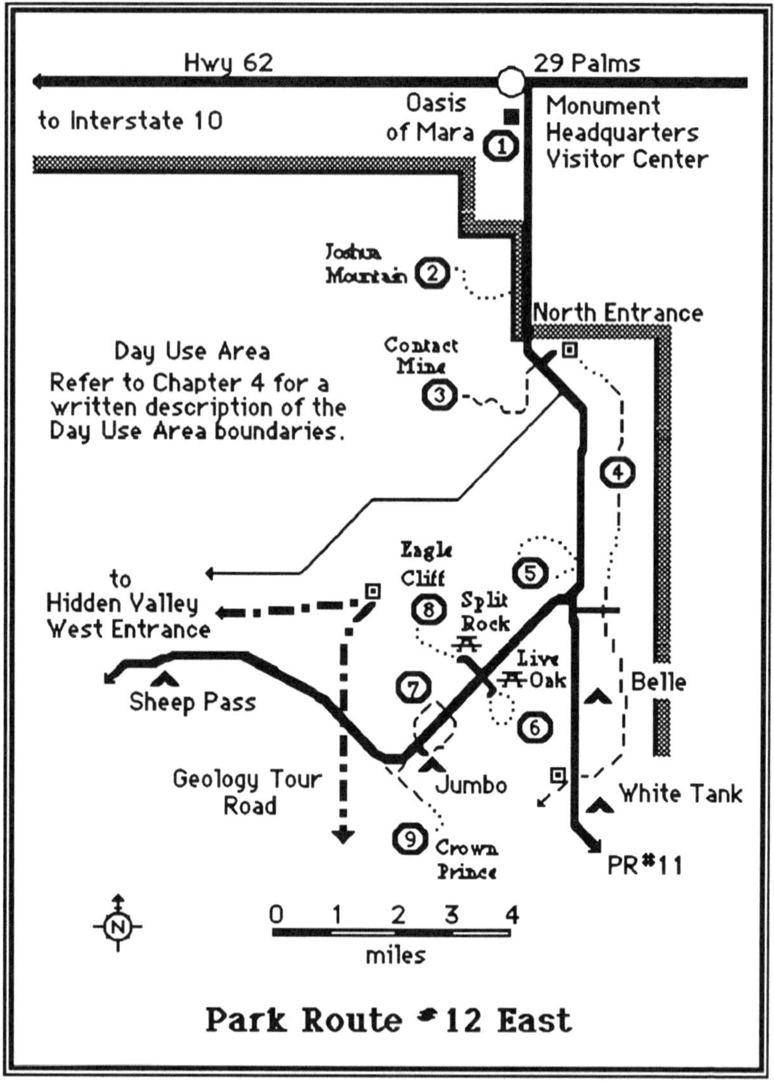


Route: Twenty-five yards north of the exhibit, an obscure dirt road leaves the west side of Park Route #12. Follow the road 1/4 mile south to a dirt dike. Cross the dike and travel 50 yards to another dike which parallels a wash. Follow the dike SW to its end. Take the right fork in the wash and continue to follow the wash as it contours around the rocky hills to the right (north). (Begin looking for a road on the lower half of the mountain to the west; it's the Contact Mine Road.)

A half mile beyond the end of the dike, the mine road leaves the right side of the wash. Watch for the road's vague beginnings at a narrow point in the wash located between two rocky hills. The first few hundred feet of the road are hard to discern. The remainder of the road is easy to follow. (Note: The road-trail to Contact Mine is not pictured on the Queen Mtn. 7.5' map; however, the mine itself is labeled. See Map # 2, Appendix D.)

## 4. CALIFORNIA RIDING AND HIKING TRAIL

(See Chapter 11)

## 5. PINTO WYE ARRASTRA

**Type**: x-country, day
**Mileage**: 1.25 miles (or 2 mile loop)
**Time**: 1 hour
**Difficulty**: moderately strenuous (loop difficult)
**Elevation Extremes**: 3550' (3440') - 3740' **Difference:** 190' (300')
**Starting and Ending Point**: pullout on PR #12, 0.5 miles north of Pinto Wye
**Topo Maps**: Queen Mtn. 7.5'

Summary: The Pinto Wye Arrastra is one of only two wagon wheel arrastras found on national park lands. It remains relatively well preserved. Because it provides an example of 19th and early 20th century ore-milling techniques, it has been nominated for placement on the

National Register of Historic Places. A more difficult, but interesting, loop hike can be made by following the wash past the mine/mill site.

Route: Park in the circular pullout located on the east side of the road, 0.5 miles north of Pinto Wye. Head west up a gully to a pass between two roadside hills. Start down the other side of the pass and look west to locate the arrastra slightly above the east side of the wash. Either return via the same route or continue on the loop hike.

To travel the loop, follow the wash NW as it winds through a boulder canyon. Upon exiting the canyon, leave the wash to the right and travel around the base of the hill. Intersect Park Route #12 and continue to the right (south) to reach the parking area. (See Map # 2, Appendix D.)

## 6. LIVE OAK / IVANPAH TANKS

**Type:** x-country / road-trail, day
**Mileage**: 1 mile loop
**Time**: 0.5 hour
**Difficulty**: easy
**Elevation Extremes:** relatively level
**Starting and Ending Point**: Live Oak Picnic Area, west end
**Topo Maps:** Queen Mtn. 7.5' , Malapai Hill 7.5'

Summary: A short loop hike travels past a very large, rare hybrid oak (after which the picnic area was named) and down a sandy, rock-enclosed wash to Live Oak Tank and then on to Ivanpah Tank. A tank is a watering hole found behind a man-made wall that spans the width of a wash. Ivanpah Tank, one of the larger tanks in the area, was built for cattle-raising in the early 1900's.

Unlike many of the other tanks in the monument, Ivanpah holds water in the wet seasons. And when the water subsides, a field of sacred daturas flourishes in the damp soil. The large trumpet shape flowers of the datura, also known as jimsonweed and thorn apple, usually bloom at night and wither in the direct sunlight. However, when there is sufficient cloud cover or shading, the flowers will continue to bloom well into the day. Fall is an excellent time to view the floral display at Ivanpah. Traveling down the wash past the tank leads to more interesting rocky terrain.

Route: Follow the sandy wash south past the large oak. The first low stone wall is Live Oak Tank. Ivanpah, a much larger tank, is farther down the same wash. At Ivanpah climb the left bank, which overlooks the tank, and locate the road-trail. The road-trail leads to the east end of the picnic area. Complete the circuit by following the picnic area road back to the west end where the hike started. (See Map # 2, Appendix D.)

*A hiker admires the large, rare oak in Live Oak Wash*

## 7. SKULL ROCK NATURE TRAIL

(See Chapter 5, Hike # 6.)

## 8. EAGLE CLIFF HILLS / MINE

**Type**: x-country, day
**Mileage**: 2.5 miles
**Time**: 2 - 3 hours
**Difficulty**: strenuous, moderately difficult
**Elevation Extremes**: 4280' - 4600' **Difference**: 320'
**Starting and Ending Point**: Split Rock Picnic Area (4280')
**Topo Maps**: Queen Mtn. 7.5'

Summary: The Eagle Cliff Hills form a beautiful and isolated wilderness fortress with rocky peaks, massive boulder piles, plentiful vegetation, and high viewpoints. Although the area is close to roads, it receives little use due to the rugged terrain. Because this area is rugged and confusing, solo travel is discouraged. Good map and compass skills are essential, especially for the return trip from the mine to Split Rock. These hills can be accessed either through Split Rock Picnic Area or through Desert Queen Mine (see Chapter 8, Hike # 9).

The Eagle Cliff Mine lies on a sheltered plateau in the heart of the Eagle Cliff Hills. The highlight of this mining area is a house built within a pile of giant boulders. The house utilizes these boulders for its walls and a portion of the roof. The remainder of the roof is constructed of dead boughs and flattened tin cans. Inside the shelter there are miscellaneous utensils, a fireplace, an iron oventop, and wooden shelves surrounding a six-pane glass window. These remnants hint about life in the early mining days.

Farther below the plateau, there are more mines and the remains of what appears to have been a blacksmith's cabin and forge. There is little known about the history of any of the structures. However, the remains indicate that a small group of miners probably lived at the Eagle Cliff Mine for an extended period of time.

This plateau is one of many good camping spots within the Eagle Cliff Hills. Overnight users need to leave from the Pine City Backcountry Board; see Chapter 8. (The mines should be considered dangerous; maintain a safe distance from the openings. Refer to Chapter 3, "Hazards - Use Caution.")

Route: Follow the paved trail to the rear of the Split Rock boulder. From here head NNW over multiple low rocky ridges to reach to a gully between two mountain points. Look for a short spire with a broad base located at the top of the gully. The spire is an important landmark for assuring travel up the correct gully. (Visually locate the spire and gully before leaving Split Rock.)

Travel up the gully along the left side until travel looks easier on the right side. Cross to the right side of the gully and travel to the ridgetop behind a large pine tree. Drop down the other side of the ridge a short distance to a gully; then continue up the opposite side of the gully to another ridgetop -- approximately 100 yards ENE of the spire. Drop down the other side of this ridge about 25 yards. Locate a pile of white mine tailings and a horizontal mine shaft approximately ten feet deep. From the tailings pile, travel NNE and pass to the right of the nearby large boulder and to the left of the three leaning slabs. Follow a trail (approximately 40 yards) to the top of a ridge. Drop down the other side of the ridge and continue N to a small relatively open plateau.

A mine is concealed beneath an oak tree near the center of the plateau. The house within the boulders can be found along the east side of the plateau. Another rock shelter (less preserved) and fireplace can be reached by traveling 100' up the passageway located outside the window side of the house.

To reach the additional mines and blacksmith's ruins, walk along the east side of the plateau to its edge. Follow an obscure, rocky trail a short ways down through the center of a boulder gully. (Respect hikers that follow who would like to see the ruins in their present state; don't disturb any of the ruins.) See topographical map on page 36.

## 9. CROWN PRINCE LOOKOUT (4581')

**Type**: road-trail / x-country, day
**Mileage**: 3 miles
**Time**: 2 hours
**Difficulty**: moderate with short section of scrambling
**Elevation Extremes**: 4400'- 4581' **Difference:** 181'
**Starting and Ending Point**: Jumbo Rocks Entrance (4400')
**Topo Maps**: Malapai Hill 7.5'

Summary: An easy hike followed by a short scramble leads to a hilltop where a lookout tower was once perched. The lookout was an airplane warning station possibly built during World War II. Today nothing remains of the lookout except a 3'x3' cement block and some anchor points. The summit of this hill offers an excellent 360° view.

Route: From Jumbo Rocks Entrance, walk west along PR#12 about 1/4 mile. A road-trail leaves from the south side of PR#12; its entrance is blocked to vehicles by large rocks. The National Park Service has attempted to naturalize the beginning of this road-trail by transplanting native vegetation. Walk to the side of the road-trail to avoid disturbing the transplant area.

Follow this road-trail approximately 3/4 mile to a fork. Turn right at the fork and continue traveling on the road-trail until it ends at the base of a rocky hill. From here follow an obscure trail along the northeast side of the hill to a steep rocky area. A short scramble up (ten vertical feet) the rocks leads to a more obvious trail. Continue following the trail to the flat, open area on the summit. (See Map # 2, Appendix D.) Note: The Crown Prince road-trail is pictured but not labeled on the USGS topographical map.

*USGS topographical map: Queen Mtn. 7.5' (1972)*
*Eagle Cliff Hills*

# Chapter 7

# PARK ROUTE #12 WEST

The western half of Park Route #12 travels through a variety of terrain as it leads from the West Entrance to Sheep Pass. Hikes originating from this road travel to the top of high peaks, into the rugged Wonderland, up wild and lush canyons, and down quiet sandy washes that gently wind through Joshua tree forests. A backcountry board is located at Keys West Gate. Campgrounds along this section of road include Hidden Valley, Ryan, and Sheep Pass Group Campground. (See map on page 38.)

## 1. QUAIL SPRINGS ROAD-TRAIL / WASH

**Type:** road-trail/cross-country, day/overnight
**Mileage**: 7.8 miles to Quail Springs (round trip)
8.5 miles to West Entrance Wash (one-way)
**Time**: 4 - 5 hours
**Difficulty**: easy
**Elevation Extremes**: 3350' - 3979' **Difference**: 629'
**Starting Point**: Quail Springs Picnic Area (3979')
**Ending Point**: Quail Springs Picnic Area (3979') / West Entrance Wash (3800')
**Topo Maps**: Indian Cove 7.5', Joshua Tree South 7.5'

Summary: This route travels across an open valley dotted with Joshua trees, passes through a mountain gap into a large isolated basin, then follows a wash through the basin to the north boundary. A concentrated stand of Joshua trees grows at the southern end of the basin at the mouth of Smith Water Canyon. This is a picturesque place to camp.

Quail Springs can be found by locating a large rock cistern near the mountain gap. The cistern, a historic holding tank for water, is now dry. Water can usually be found trickling from the spring on the hillside above the tank. During the wetter months, a small, lush green oasis flourishes around the spring. (Don't depend on finding water at the spring for drinking.)

There is an interesting side trip not far from Quail Springs. The route leads to a collection of engraved rock slabs. A Swedish immigrant, who homesteaded the area in the early 1900's, carved his philosophical beliefs on the rocks. Ask a ranger for more information on the area. (Vandalism is a major concern for these unique, irreplaceable carvings.)

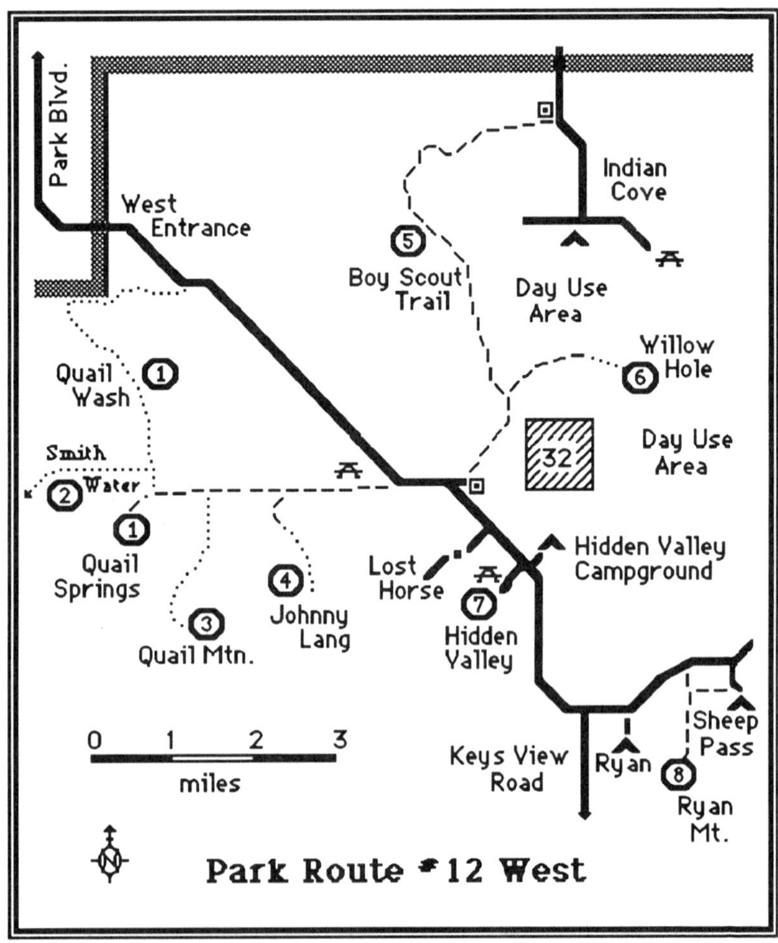


Route: Follow the road-trail west from Quail Springs Picnic Area. Watch for the point where the road-trail exits the wash on the south side, about 3/4 mile from the picnic area. (The road-trail provides easier traveling; the wash eventually heads in a different direction.) Follow the road-trail and intermittent wash until they pass through the remains of a fence. Just beyond the fence, the wash bends sharply to the right. At this point, the road-trail leaves the wash on the left side and continues straight. The road-trail, which is not easily recognizable, travels SW toward the base of the southern hills.

To reach Quail Springs, follow the road-trail as it bends to the south. Travel up through a section of fire-blackened Joshua trees. If the road-trail is lost, travel west along the base of the southern mountains; then head south up through the dead Joshua trees to the base of a rocky cirque. The cistern and spring are along the western edge of this cirque.

To continue to the north boundary, backtrack to the point where the road-trail turned south. Continue a short distance farther to access the main wash. Follow the wash northwest into the large sloping basin. (An intermittent jeep trail parallels the wash, but it is difficult to follow.) Just before the boundary, the wash enters a canyon. A barbed wire fence spans the wash at this point. Continue past this fence about 1/4 mile to a boulder and cable fence marked with National Park Service boundary signs.

Travel right (east) along the fence toward the hills. Locate and follow the faint road-trail which parallels the fence on the south side. Continue following the road-trail east up into a side wash (West Entrance Wash). Follow the wash up through the canyon. About 1.25 miles from the fence, there is a perpendicular fork in the wash. Take the left fork and follow it 1/4 mile to PR #12. (See Map # 3 & 7, Appendix D.)

## 2. SMITH WATER CANYON - (See Chapter 13, Hike # 7.)

## 3. QUAIL MOUNTAIN (5813')

**Type**: road-trail/x-country, day/overnight
**Mileage**: 12 miles
**Time**: 7 - 9 hours
**Difficulty**: strenuous, difficult
**Elevation Extremes**: 3680' - 5813' **Difference**: 2133'
**Starting and Ending Point**: Quail Springs Picnic Area (3979')
**Topo Maps**: Indian Cove 7.5', Joshua Tree South 7.5'

Summary: This beautiful hike leads up through an unlikely verdant canyon to the summit of the highest peak in the monument. The narrow canyon contains thick grasses, rushes, and trees growing among water-streaked rocks and clear pools (seasonal). It is a surprising contrast to the surrounding dry desert and stark, fire-blackened summit of Quail. The lush canyon is susceptible to impact; please tread lightly and make overnight camps only at the drier base of the canyon or on the broad summit.

As can be expected, there is an excellent circular view from the summit. A climbing register is located near the large cairn that marks the summit. (Note: This is a confusing route. It is easy to get off-track and end up on one of the surrounding peaks. See Chapter 10 for an easier route to the summit.)

Route: Follow Quail Springs Road-Trail approximately three miles. Head south up the second wide valley (the first is Johnny Lang Canyon). This valley funnels into a narrow canyon. Quail Mountain is the broad rounded mountain centered above this valley and canyon. Follow the main wash up through the narrow canyon. The canyon forks several times; stay in the large, main wash. When a fork in the canyon results in two washes of apparently equal size, take the left wash.

Travel becomes more difficult in the upper reaches of the canyon. Some difficult boulder scrambling and short sections of low-angle slab climbing (class III) will be encountered. The wash forks again at a higher, fire-scarred, more open section of the mountain. Take the left fork and follow the wash to an open, flat area. The summit is up to the east. (Note: The high peaks surrounding Quail are pointed -- a contrast to Quail's large, rounded, almost flat summit. This fact should help eliminate some confusion.) (See Map # 7, Appendix D.)

## 4. JOHNNY LANG CANYON / MINE / VIEWPOINT

**Type**: road-trail/x-country, day/overnight
**Mileage**: 10.5 miles round trip to end of canyon
9 miles round trip to mine
7.5 miles round trip to viewpoint
**Time:** 6 - 7 hours
**Difficulty**: canyon -- moderate, moderately difficult
(mine -- strenuous, viewpoint -- moderately strenuous)
**Elevation Extremes**: 3979' - 4400' (mine -- 4800', viewpoint -- 4380')
**Difference**: 421' (821', 401')
**Starting and Ending Point**: Quail Springs Picnic Area (3979')
**Topo Maps**: Indian Cove 7.5'

Summary: This hike offers a variety of terrain, vegetation, and views. Johnny Lang Canyon is named after the early prospector who began the Lost Horse Mine operations. After Johnny sold his shares in the Lost Horse Mine, he moved into a small cabin in this canyon and worked his mining claim in the hills above his little house. The scanty remains of his cabin can be found at the mouth of the canyon. The mine shafts remain as Johnny left them. (The mines are unstable and dangerous; maintain a safe distance from their openings. Refer to Chapter 3, "Hazards - Use Caution.")

Quiet beauty was probably an important aspect that drew Lang to this particular canyon. It is still an isolated and beautiful place. Many large pinyon pines grow in the rugged, rocky valley of the upper canyon. Small pools of water can sometimes be found in the sandy and rocky washes. At the cabin site near the mouth of the canyon, clear water (seasonal and intermittent) flows down the rocky wash. From the mine, located at 4800', and approach ridges, there are good views of the Wonderland of Rocks and the surrounding valley.

A scenic side trip from the cabin site leads up (300' in elevation) along the east side of the canyon. This old prospector trail steadily and rapidly climbs to a high vantage point. The route passes an impressive collection of pancake and barrel cacti high up on the rocky slopes. The trail, which originates near the cabin, was probably used by Johnny Lang himself as a means to reach mines on the other side of the mountain.

Route: Follow the road-trail west from Quail Springs Picnic Area approximately 2 miles. (Watch for the point where the road-trail exits the wash on the south side, about 3/4 mile from the picnic area.) Turn south on a road-trail that leads up the first large valley. From here, either travel up the wash or along the road-trail. (The road-trail becomes faint and difficult to follow in spots.)

The meager remains of Johnny's cabin are at the end of this road-trail. Look for these ruins above and 50' to the right (west) of the wash just before the point where the wash enters the narrowed canyon. Continue up the rocky wash to attain the upper valley. A short section of difficult scrambling leads to the uppermost part of the valley. This difficult section can be avoided by leaving the right side of the wash (just before the difficult section) and traveling up between two rocky knolls. Climbing over the ridge at the southern end of Johnny Lang Canyon will lead to Lost Horse Valley. (Note: Private properties are located near this section of Lost Horse Valley. Respect the landowners' rights; do not trespass.) See Map # 3, Appendix D.

Johnny Lang Mine: To reach the mine, continue 1/2 mile up the wash from the cabin site. Climb up a knoll on the south (right) side of the wash. The mining trail that ascends the knoll is barely visible. (This knoll can be identified when the canyon opens and a distant, high rounded mountain -- set back from the right side of the wash -- becomes visible. The knoll is close to the wash and left of this mountain.) From the top of this knoll, look south across a side canyon to locate the mine tailings amidst a thick section of pine and oak trees. A mining trail which leads up to the mine is also visible at this point.

Viewpoint: From the cabin site, look across the wash and up the hillside. There is a large rock cairn located on the hillside (at 95°) about 250 yards away. (The cairn which blends in with the rocky hillside is difficult to spot.) The cairn marks the prospector trail. From the cairn, follow the faint, narrow, rocky trail southeast up the mountainside. The trail disappears at the saddle on the south side of the mountain. (Note: This trail is not maintained; use caution while travelling across the steep slopes.)

## 5. BOY SCOUT TRAIL

**Type**: trail, day/overnight
**Mileage**: 8 miles one-way
**Time**: 4 - 5 hours
**Difficulty**: moderate
**Elevation Extremes**: 2840' - 4160' **Difference**: 1320'
**Starting Point**: Keys West Gate (4040')
**Ending Point:** Indian Cove Backcountry Board (2840')
**Topo Maps**: Indian Cove 7.5'

Summary: The Boy Scout Trail provides a variety of terrain and views. It is fairly easy to follow and travels mostly downhill from Keys West Gate to Indian Cove. The first portion of the trail leads along the edge of the Wonderland of Rocks and follows picturesque, sandy washes lined with junipers, pinyon pines, and oak trees. The latter portion of the trail travels along a rocky mountainside; winds through steep mountains and narrow canyons; and then continues through the open desert to Indian Cove. There are many good places for camping not far from the trail. Small backpacking parties will enjoy camping near sandy washes shaded by the large trees and rocks -- approximately 3.5 miles from the trailhead. Note: Camping is only allowed on the west side of the trail. (Be aware of flash flood danger when camping near washes.)

Route: Follow the trail (1.4 miles) north from the parking area to a fork marked with a sign "Horse and Foot Trail." Take the trail to the left. This trail is blazed with metal posts marked with two white bands. Approximately four miles from the trailhead, the trail makes a sharp left turn out of a wash. This turn may be poorly identified. Missing the turn will result in travel into a steep, nearly impassable canyon. To prevent this error, watch for a tank (a man-made wall that spans the width of the wash) and water trough. A short distance beyond the trough, the trail leaves the wash and heads west (left). The remainder of the trail should pose no problem. (Note: This trail is pictured on topographical maps. However, both the first mile and the last mile of the trail have been rerouted since the topographical maps were printed.) This trail is also commonly hiked from Indian Cove uphill to Keys West Gate. (See Map # 3 & 6, Appendix D.)

## 6. WILLOW HOLE / WONDERLAND

(See Chapter 16, Hike # 3.)

## 7. HIDDEN VALLEY NATURE TRAIL

(See Chapter 5, Hike # 2.)

*The Hidden Valley Trail lies at the base of high, rocky walls*

## 8. RYAN MOUNTAIN (5457')

**Type:** trail, day
**Mileage:** 3 miles
**Time:** 2 - 3 hours
**Difficulty:** moderately strenuous
**Elevation Extremes:** 4480' - 5457' **Difference:** 977'
**Starting and Ending Point:** Ryan Mt. Parking Area (4480')
**Topo Maps:** Key's View 7.5', Indian Cove 7.5'

Summary: The Ryan Mountain trail and summit provide some of the best panoramic views in the park. From the summit, there is a 360° view of the monument. The view includes Mt. San Jacinto, Mt. San Gorgonio, most of the monument valleys, Pinto Basin, the Wonderland of Rocks, and more. The trail travels continuously uphill; it is well-maintained and easy to follow.

While traveling up the trail, look west to the rock formation known as Saddle Rocks and watch for rock climbers. The longest technical

*The view from Ryan Mountain includes Mt. San Jacinto, the Little San Bernardino Mountains, and Lost Horse Valley*

climbing routes in the monument are located on this formation. (See Map # 3, Appendix D.)

Alternative Start: A spur trail leaves from Sheep Pass Campground from both Site #1 and across the road from Site #6. Leaving from Sheep Pass adds 1.5 miles round trip. The spur trail joins the main trail just above the Ryan Mt. Parking Area.

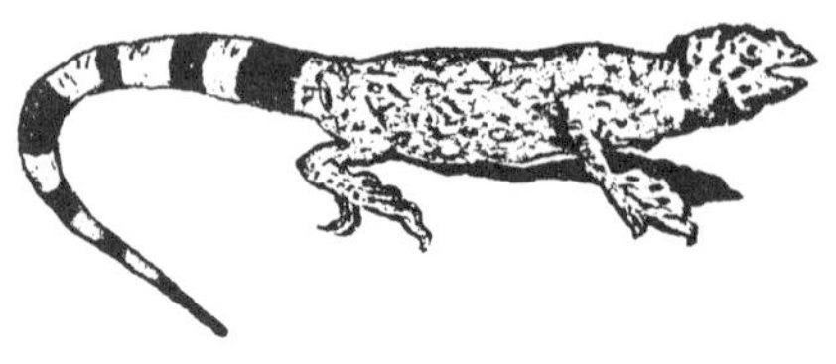

# Chapter 8

# QUEEN VALLEY

Queen Valley contains one of the larger Joshua tree forests in the monument. The valley is bounded by mountains to the north and Pleasant Valley to the south. A system of dirt roads travels through the center of Queen Valley. These roads are a starting point for several hikes to areas of both natural and historic interest. The dirt roads can be accessed at three locations -- a dirt road heading east out of Hidden Valley Campground; a northwest-bound road which departs Park Route #12 east of Sheep Pass; and a road leading north off Park Route #12, 1.7 miles west of Jumbo Rocks Campground. The Pine City Backcountry Board is located in the northeast corner of this road system. (See map on page 46.)

## 1. THE BIG BARKER DAM LOOP

**Type**: trail/road-trail, day
**Mileage**: 3 mile loop
**Time:** 2 hours
**Difficulty**: easy, easy scrambling
**Elevation Extremes**: fairly level
**Starting and Ending Point**: Bulletin Board, Loop C , Hidden Valley Camp
**Topo Maps**: Indian Cove 7.5'

Summary: This hike is an extension of the Barker Dam Nature Trail. The route travels past the educational exhibits and historical sites located along the nature trail. However, this longer loop expands upon the nature trail loop by adding distance and a greater variety of terrain and scenery.

The trail travels across the open desert from Hidden Valley Campground to Barker Dam where it intersects the nature trail. The hike continues around the nature trail then returns to the campground on a route which winds through large rock formations. Watch for rock climbers along the way. These rock formations are well known for having many popular climbing routes. For a complete description of the Barker Dam area, refer to Chapter 5, Hike # 3.

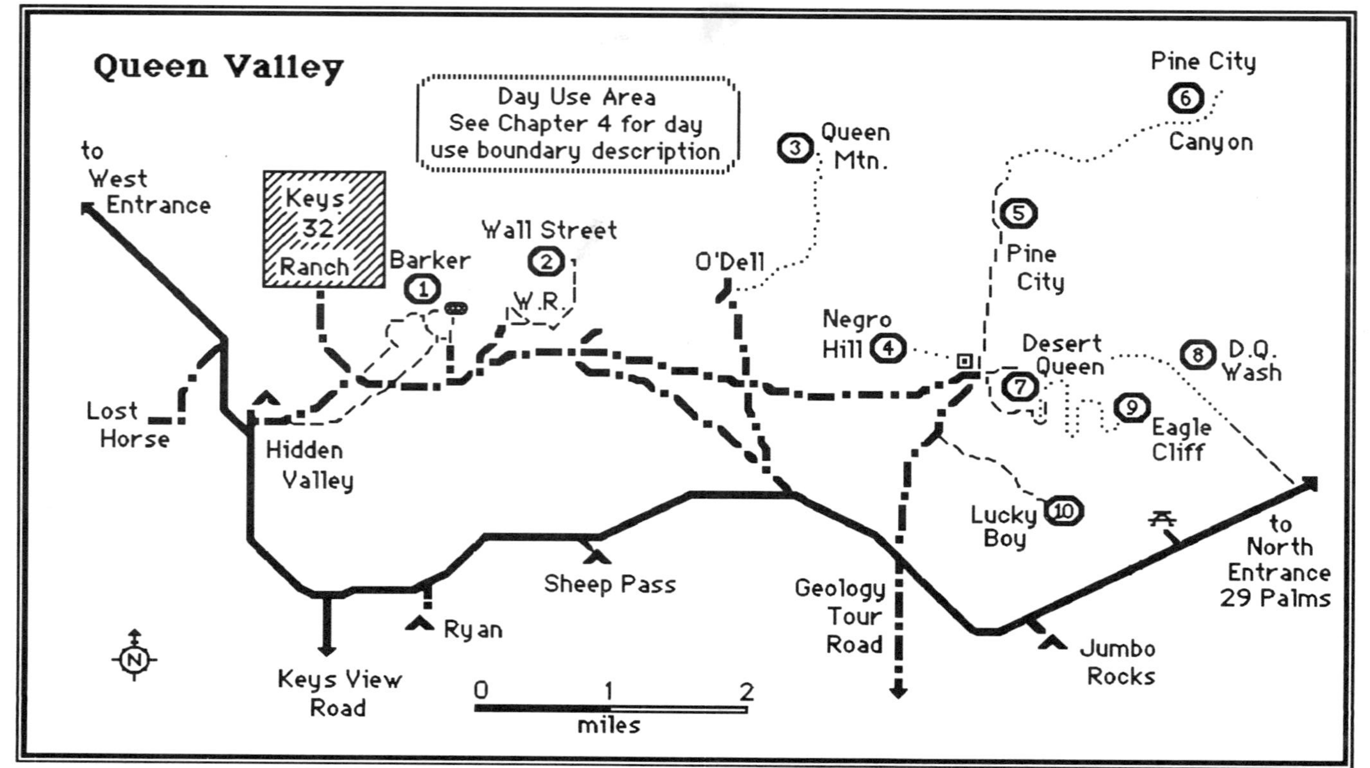
Queen Valley
Day Use Area
See Chapter 4 for day
use boundary description
to West Entrance
Keys 32 Ranch
Barker 1
Wall Street 2
W.R.
O'Dell
3 Queen Mtn.
Pine City
6
Canyon
5 Pine City
Negro Hill 4
Desert Queen 7
8 D.Q. Wash
9 Eagle Cliff
Lost Horse
Hidden Valley
Lucky Boy 10
to North Entrance 29 Palms
Sheep Pass
Geology Tour Road
Ryan
Keys View Road
Jumbo Rocks
0
1
2
miles
N

Route: Follow the trail northeast from the bulletin board to a dirt road. Cross the dirt road and continue on the trail to reach a wash. Follow the wash east about 200 yards to a fence. Travel north along the fence toward the rocks to locate the continuing trail. A short distance beyond the fence, the trail is marked by posts with directional arrows. Follow the marked trail to the Disney Petroglyphs. Continue 100 feet beyond the petroglyphs and turn right (east) at the junction. The trail leads to the Barker Dam Parking Lot.

Continue to follow the nature trail north to the dam. From the base of the dam, follow the trail about 1/4 mile to a junction. At this point, a directional arrow will indicate an abrupt left turn. However, don't turn left; instead, travel down the road-trail to the right. Travel another 1/4 mile and turn left at a fork. Continue about 1/2 mile to the next fork, turn right, and follow the trail out to Echo "T" intersection. From here, hike southwest down the dirt road and back to the bulletin board. (See Map # 3, Appendix D.)

## 2. WALL STREET MILL

**Type**: road-trail, day
**Mileage**: 1.5 miles
**Time:** 1 hour
**Difficulty**: easy
**Elevation Extremes**: 4280' - 4340' **Difference:** 60'
**Starting and Ending Point**: Wonderland Ranch Parking Area (4280')
**Topo Maps**: Indian Cove 7.5'

Summary: Wall Street Mill was owned by Bill Keys. He used the mill to process ore from the Desert Queen Mine. Wall Street is not the largest mill in the monument, but it is well preserved and is, therefore, an important part of the monument's history.

Look for a stone marker on the way to the mill. The stone reads, "Here is Where Worth Bagly Bit the dust At the HAND of W.F. KEYS, May 11, 1943." Bagley was killed in a shootout with Keys in a controversy over the use of the road. After spending five years in prison, Keys was found not-guilty; it was determined that he shot in self-defense.

Surrounding the mill, there are several old cars, trucks, and pieces of machinery -- more reminders of the early mining days. The mill is located in a picturesque area on the edge of the Wonderland. Traveling in the wash past the mill will lead into a rocky maze vegetated with oak, manzanita, and jojoba.

Route: From the parking area, follow the road-trail approximately 50 yards to a fork. From here, either follow the left (NW) fork toward the remains of a pink ranch house, or bypass the house by continuing NE (right fork) on a less-traveled road-trail. (A short distance farther, the two road-trails join back together. There is an old model truck located just NW of the point where the two trails rejoin.) The road-trail continues to a windmill and the Desert Queen Well. It bends to the east around the windmill, passes through the remains of a barbed-wire fence, then makes a hairpin turn. The "shootout" stone is on the left side of the road-trail past the hairpin turn. The road-trail eventually narrows to the size of a path. At this point, begin looking to the left (west) for the mill. (See Map # 3, Appendix D.)

## 3. QUEEN MOUNTAIN (5687')

**Type**: x-country, day/overnight (note day use area)
**Mileage**: 4 miles
**Time**: 3 - 4 hours
**Difficulty**: strenuous, moderately difficult
**Elevation Extremes**: 4480' - 5687' **Difference:** 1207'
**Starting and Ending Point**: O'Dell Parking Area (4480')
**Topo Maps**: Queen Mtn. 7.5'

Summary: Queen Mountain is the most prominent peak in Queen Valley. A short hike through a wash, followed by a rugged climb up a trail-less mountainside, leads to good views of the Wonderland of Rocks, Queen and Lost Horse valleys, and distant Mt. San Gorgonio. Desert Bighorn Sheep are occasionally seen on the slopes of Queen Mountain or on the rocky peaks directly to the north. Golden Eagles can sometimes be seen flying near the cliffs on these mountains.

Queen Mountain is located within a day use area. However, camping is allowed near the south base of the mountain outside the restricted area. Overnight users need to start from the Pine City Backcountry Board; this will make the trip longer and less direct. A climbing register is located on the summit.

*A rugged climb up a gully (center of picture) leads to the summit of Queen Mountain -- the pointed peak pictured left center*

Route: From O'Dell Parking Area, head east (< 1/4 mile) to the second sandy wash. Travel up the wash, which heads generally northeast. Follow the wash through some low hills and on to the base of the mountain near an obvious slide area. Continue following the wash (now rocky) up a steep rocky grade. Follow the wash as it makes a sharp turn to the west. (Rocky cliffs stretch across the mountain above this point.) A hundred yards further, the route departs from the wash (as marked on the topographical maps) and continues NNW up an obvious route -- a rocky gully with steep sides. The gully opens up near the summit. Climb up along the right side of the gully (near the base of the cliffs). Continue to the ridge between the two high summits -- 5687' and 5677'. From the ridge, head west to the higher of the two points. A large slab leads to the summit. The climbing register is located within a pile of rocks and under a large dead tree limb. (See Map # 3, Appendix D.)

## 4. NEGRO HILL (4875')

**Type**: x-country, day
**Mileage**: 1.5 miles
**Time**: 1.5 hours
**Difficulty**: moderately strenuous
**Elevation Extremes**: 4436' - 4875' **Difference**: 439'
**Starting and Ending Point**: Pine City Backcountry Board (4436')
**Topo Maps**: Queen Mtn. 7.5'

Summary: A seemingly unremarkable hill stands alone on the eastern edge of Queen Valley. This hill, known as Negro Hill, may look uninteresting from the base; however, the short hike to the summit is well worth the effort. The 360° view from the summit includes Mt. San Jacinto, Mt. San Gorgonio, Queen Valley, Quail Mountain, Pine City, Eagle Cliff Hills, the Wonderland, distant mountain ranges to the south and east, and more. The open summit provides a good vantage point for enjoying the colorful desert sunsets. (Use care when descending the hill in low light; there is no trail and the ground is rocky.)

Route: Negro Hill is the obvious hill located a short distance west of the backcountry board. Head west up any likely slope. (Map # 2, Appendix D.)

## 5. PINE CITY

**Type**: road-trail, day/overnight (note day use area)
**Mileage**: 3 miles
**Time:** 2 hours
**Difficulty**: easy
**Elevation Extremes**: 4436' - 4560' **Difference:** 124'
**Starting and Ending Point**: Pine City Backcountry Board (4436')
**Topo Maps**: Queen Mtn. 7.5'

Summary: It takes less than an hour to hike to Pine City, but it can take more than a day to explore and enjoy the quiet solitude of this pretty area. The area was not a city or town. At most, there were one or two small cabins which are now gone. A few caved-in mine shafts are the only remains of this small mining area. However, it is the island of desert greenery, and not the history, that draws hikers to this area. Large pine trees grow among an isolated collection of rocky walls and boulder mounds. This is an excellent place for bird watching. Bighorn sheep are known to inhabit the area, particularly in the summer months. Most of Pine City lies just inside the day use area, but camping is allowed on the southern edge of the area.

Route: An easy-to-follow road-trail leaves from the west side of the parking lot. Follow the road-trail 1.5 miles to Pine City. A trail branches off the road-trail on the right (east) side, 0.7 miles from the parking lot. It leads up to a ridge and the remains of a mining camp. The other trails that are marked on the topographical map are overgrown and difficult or impossible to follow. (See Map # 2, Appendix D.)

## 6. PINE CITY CANYON

**Type**: road-trail/x-country, day/overnight (note day use area)
**Mileage**: 5.5 miles one way
**Time**: 4 hours
**Difficulty**: moderate, difficult
**Elevation Extremes**: 2920' - 4580' **Difference**: 1660'
**Starting Point**: Pine City Backcountry Board (4436')
**Ending Point**: North Entrance Exhibit (2920')
**Topo Maps**: Queen Mtn. 7.5'

Summary: A hike down Pine City Canyon provides an adventuresome addition to the Pine City hike. This hike affords the opportunity to enjoy both the gentle quiet of Pine City and some interesting boulder scrambling in the canyon. After leaving Pine City, the route follows a wash down through a narrow, steep-sided canyon. Easy wash walking is intermixed with several sections of moderate to difficult boulder scrambling. In addition, there are a couple of short 15' sections of class III (see glossary) down climbing.

The lower half of the canyon is brightened by colorful rocks. The shades of pink, orange, red, and yellow are the natural results of mineral presence.

Route: Upon reaching Pine City, follow the road-trail to the left (NW) of the boulder piles. The road-trail (marked on the topographical map) continues past several mine shafts and ends on a ridge. (Climb to the top of the knoll (NW) for views down into Twentynine Palms Valley and beyond.) From the end of the road, drop NE down over the ridge. Follow the gully down to the north to intersect the canyon wash. Travel northeast down the canyon. Upon exiting the canyon, continue to follow the wash 1.5 miles to intersect Park Route #12 near the North Entrance Exhibit. (Map # 2, Appendix D.)

## 7. DESERT QUEEN MINE

**Type**: trail, day
**Mileage**: 1.2 miles of trail,
**Time**: 1 hour,
**Difficulty**: easy - moderate,
**Elevation Extremes**: 4300' - 4440' **Difference:** 140'
**Starting and Ending Points**: Pine City Backcountry Board (4436')
**Topo Maps**: Queen Mtn. 7.5'

Summary: The Desert Queen Mine was one of the most profitable and longest operating mines in the monument area. According to the US Bureau of Mines, it produced 3,845 ounces of gold which, in turn, yielded several million dollars. Machinery, stone building ruins, and several mine shafts dot the hillsides in a concentrated area above the Desert Queen Wash. Today most of the shafts are blocked by steel grates through which can be seen the structure of the shafts and some equipment that was used within the mines.

Route: The main trail (easy) leads from the east side of the parking lot, passes building ruins, and continues to an overlook above the major part of the mining area. A second trail (moderate) departs the main trail 200 yards beyond the parking lot. This trail travels south down into a sandy ravine and up the other side where most of the mines are located. (See topographical map on page 36.)

## 8. DESERT QUEEN WASH

**Type**: trail/x-country, day
**Mileage**: 3.5 miles (one way)
**Time**: 2-3 hours
**Difficulty**: moderate, moderately difficult
**Elevation Extremes**: 3875' - 4440' **Difference:** 565'
**Starting Point**: Pine City Backcountry Board (4436')
**Ending Point**: PR#12, two paved pullouts, 1 mile west of Pinto Wye (3884')
**Topo Maps**: Queen Mtn. 7.5'

Summary: The walk down Desert Queen Wash is a pleasant addition to the Desert Queen Mine hike (preceding hike). The sandy wash travels east through a ravine lined with large oak, juniper, willows, and pine trees. There is some moderate boulder scrambling in the lower half of the wash. The wash passes John's Camp, the Ming Mine (circa 1931), and other pioneer mining encampments as it continues downhill for three miles. At John's Camp, the route leaves the wash and follows a road-trail across relatively flat terrain to Park Route #12.

Route: Follow the Desert Queen Mine trail south down into a sandy ravine. Travel down the ravine which leads generally north and then east. The first significant mining encampment is located about 1.5 miles down the wash. To locate this site, watch for the remains of a model T pickup truck which sits above the wash about 50' beyond the right bank. The cabin remains are located 75' down the wash from the truck on the southeast side of a large boulder.

To locate John's Camp, continue down the wash another 1/2 mile to the Ming Mine. (The mine shafts are dangerous; maintain a safe distance from their openings. Refer to Chapter 3, "Hazards-Use Caution.") Watch for the bluish gray tailings pile up on the left bank about 50' above the wash. From the mine, continue 400' down the wash and exit the wash on the right side. John's Camp is located in this area between the wash and the bottom of the ridge. Look for the cement platform, scattered metal debris, rock inscriptions, and a metal and rock stove.

Locate the overgrown road-trail which parallels the bottom of the ridge. Follow the road-trail southeast then south (right) around the nose of the ridge. The road-trail disappears in a wash. Travel up the wash about 100 yards. At this point the wash bends around the ridge and heads west. The road-trail heads south up a less obvious drainage. (Look beyond the row of bushes to spot the continuing road-trail.) The road-trail travels 100' up this drainage then heads ESE up over the bank. The remainder of the road-trail is fairly easy to follow. Travel southeast down the road-trail and exit onto Park Route #12 between the two paved pullouts. (See Map # 2, Appendix D.)

## 9. EAGLE CLIFF MINE

**Type:** x-country, day/overnight
**Mileage**: 4.5 miles
**Time**: 3 - 4 hours
**Difficulty**: strenuous, moderately difficult
**Elevation Extremes**: 4300' - 4733' **Difference:** 433'
**Starting and Ending Point**: Pine City Backcountry Board (4436')
**Topo Maps**: Queen Mtn. 7.5'

Summary: See Chapter 6, Hike # 8, Eagle Cliff Hills/Mine, for a complete summary. Travel to Eagle Cliff Mine via this route is longer, more rugged, and has more route-finding difficulty than the route which leaves from Split Rock.

Route: Follow the trail from the parking area to the wash below Desert Queen Mine (see preceding hike). Travel NW down the sandy wash. As the wash starts bending to the NE, distant hills will become visible

*Excellent views can be obtained from the Eagle Cliff Hills*

above the wash. Continue down the wash 50 yards from this point then head SE up a gully. When the gully begins to level out, look above the left side of the gully for the built-up banking of an old mining road (below a short, rocky cliff section). Continue up the gully to meet this road.

Travel the obscure road up to the north and continue following it as it contours around and beneath a boulder-covered hilltop. The road drops into a sandy wash 1/2 mile from the point where the road was first picked up. From the wash, look SE and locate a rock spire at the top of a rocky gully. Travel up the gully to a point just below the ridgetop -- approximately 100 yards to the left (northeast) of the spire. (The mining road, which is difficult to locate and follow, travels up the left side of this gully. An obscure trail zigzags up the final steep section to the ridgetop.)

Find the pile of white mine tailings and the mine shaft located just below the ridgetop (north side). See Chapter 6, Hike # 8 for the remainder of the route description. (Refer to topographical map on page 36.)

## 10. LUCKY BOY VISTA

**Type:** road-trail, day/overnight
**Mileage**: 2.5 miles
**Time**: 2 hours
**Difficulty**: easy
**Elevation Extremes**: 4430' - 4520' **Difference:** 90'
**Starting and Ending Point**: Lucky Boy Junction (4430')
**Topo Maps**: Queen Mtn. 7.5'

Summary: The hike to Lucky Boy Vista is an excellent choice for an easy overnight trip as well as for a good day trip. The trail leads to a high level plateau which provides both superb views and some fine places to camp. The trail travels through the eastern edge of Queen Valley, winds around through a few large boulders, then climbs a short distance up through some hills to reach the high plateau. From the plateau, there are good views of the rocky Eagle Cliff Hills and views down into the rugged drainages which lead north to Desert Queen Mine.

The road-trail ends at an overlook above the Split Rock boulder formation maze. The Elton Mine, which consists of several vertical shafts (the majority of which are fenced), is also located at the end of the road-trail. (The mine shafts are dangerous; maintain a safe distance from their openings. Refer to Chapter 3, "Hazards-Use Caution.")

At one time, a road-trail connected the Elton Mine with the Split Rock Road. Now the trail is mostly overgrown. However, with a discerning eye and good map and compass skills, it is possible to locate and follow the majority of this connecting route.

Route: From the parking area, follow the road-trail east to the overlook. For overnight trips, park at the Pine City Backcountry Board and follow the road south to the Lucky Boy Junction. Leaving from the backcountry board adds about one round trip mile to the hike. (The road-trail is marked on 15' topographical maps but not on 7.5' maps.) See Map # 2, Appendix D.

# Chapter 9

# GEOLOGY TOUR ROAD

The Geology Tour Road is an eighteen-mile (round trip) dirt road. A pamphlet, obtained at the beginning of the road, interprets the geology of the area. Numbered markers at pullouts along the road correspond to numbers in the pamphlet. The road travels from Queen Valley down a long alluvial fan to a one-way loop around the perimeter of Pleasant Valley. A rough road branches off the southeast corner of the loop. This side road travels through Berdoo Canyon to Dillon Road, which parallels the southern boundary of the monument. (Note: Portions of Berdoo Canyon are frequently impassable, even with four-wheel drive vehicles.)

The Geology Tour Road begins at Park Route #12, five miles west of Pinto Wye and 2.4 miles east of Sheep Pass. Four-wheel drive vehicles are recommended, especially for travel on the lower section of the one-way loop. However, if the roads are dry, two-wheel drive vehicles can usually travel the entire road without difficulty. Inquire about road conditions at a visitor center before attempting the drive.

Hikes starting from the Geology Tour Road travel through broad valleys forested with Joshua trees, down long sandy washes that wind through steep canyons, or up rocky gullies that lead to mountain peaks and high vistas. Unique geologic formations and sites of historical interest are additional hike highlights. Backcountry boards are located 1.4 miles and 6.8 miles from Park Route #12. The latter board is in Pleasant Valley. The closest campground is Jumbo Rocks, 1.6 miles east on Park Route #12.

## 1. CALIFORNIA RIDING AND HIKING TRAIL

(See Chapter 11)

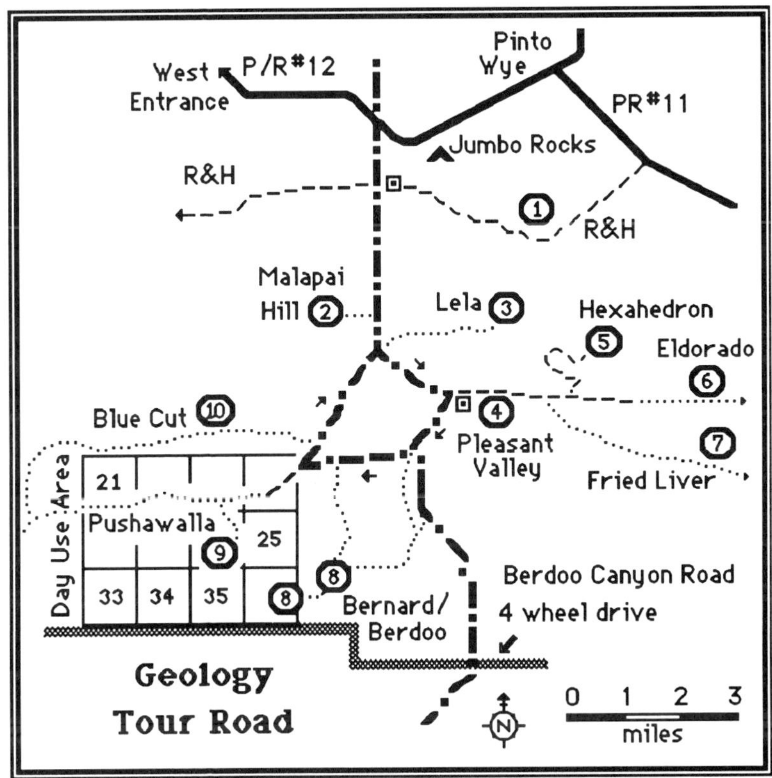


## 2. MALAPAI HILL (4280')

**Type**: x-country, day
**Mileage**: 1.5 miles
**Time**: 1 - 2 hours
**Difficulty**: moderately strenuous, moderately difficult
**Elevation Extremes**: 3760' - 4280' **Difference:** 520'
**Starting and Ending Point**: Stop #7 (3760')
**Topo Maps**: Malapai Hill 7.5'

Summary: This is a good hike for geology enthusiasts. Malapai Hill is a volcanic dome which sits alone in the lower half of Queen Valley. A large area of columnar jointing can be viewed from either the summit saddle or from the northwest side of the hill. The summit provides good views of surrounding Pleasant Valley. A slight variation of the approach route leads to a large balanced boulder.

Route: Travel WSW on relatively level ground to the base of the hill. (The balanced boulder can be seen SW from the parking area.) Attain

*The approach route to Malapai Hill passes a large monzogranite boulder*

the saddle by ascending directly up or to either side of the liver-colored scree slope. (Climbing the scree is easier than it looks from a distance. The scree is composed of large, relatively stable rocks.) The summit is the point north of the saddle. The columnar jointing is best viewed by looking down on the columnar cliff from the NW section of the saddle plateau. Use caution as rocks may be loose near the plateau edge. (See Map # 4, Appendix D.)

## 3. LELA PEAK (4747')

**Type**: x-country, day/overnight
**Mileage**: 5 miles
**Time:** 3 - 4 hours
**Difficulty**: strenuous
**Elevation Extremes**: 3520' - 4747' **Difference:** 1227'
**Starting and Ending Point**: Squaw Tank (3520')
**Topo Maps**: Malapai Hill 7.5'

Summary: Lela Peak is the highest peak in the northern Hexie Mountains. A straightforward climb leads to unobstructed views of the monument -- across Pinto Basin to the Coxcombs, across the Hexies to Monument and Eagle mountains, and across Pleasant and Queen valleys to the Wonderland of Rocks.

Route: Wind through the boulder formations just north of the parking area. Travel northeast along the north base of the mountains. Head ENE up the second deep gully (about 1.25 miles from the parking area) to a plateau. Travel NE over a low ridge to reach another broad plateau. Lela is the high point on the opposite side of this second plateau. (See Map # 4, Appendix D.)

## 4. PLEASANT VALLEY ROAD-TRAIL

**Type**: road-trail, day/overnight
**Mileage**: 5 miles
**Time:** 2 - 3 hours
**Difficulty**: easy
**Elevation Extremes**: relatively level
**Starting and Ending Point**: Pleasant Valley Backcountry Board (3250')
**Topo Maps**: Malapai Hill 7.5'

Summary: This pleasant hike travels through a flat, dry lake bed. During wet seasons, the area resembles a manicured lawn dotted with several species of desert shrubs. It is a great place for overnight camping and early-morning bird watching.

Route: The road-trail leaves from the backcountry board and heads east across the valley. Good camping spots are located throughout the valley at the base of the Hexies. (See Map # 4, Appendix D.)

## 5. HEXAHEDRON MINE

**Type**: road-trail, day/overnight
**Mileage**: 8 miles
**Time:** 5 - 6 hours
**Difficulty**: moderately strenuous
**Elevation Extremes**: 3200'- 4000' **Difference:** 800'
**Starting and Ending Point**: Pleasant Valley Backcountry Board (3250')
**Topo Maps**: Malapai Hill 7.5'

Summary: There is a variety of panoramic views from the road-trail that winds up through the mountains to the Hexahedron Mine. Although the Hexahedron Mine itself is not significant, a nearby rock house perched on the edge of a mountain makes this an interesting destination. Level camping areas with good views can be found near the roofless rock house. (The mine shafts are dangerous; maintain a safe distance from the openings. Refer to Chapter 3, "Hazards - Use Caution.")

Route: Follow the Pleasant Valley Road-Trail (see preceding hike) to a small hill. Just before the hill, the road-trail enters a wash. Cross the wash to find the continuing road-trail. Pass through a fence at the base of the hill and continue up the road-trail to a fork. From here head N to attain the obvious mining road that ascends the mountain side. This mining road is fairly easy to follow the remaining way to the mine and rock house. (Note: The trail to the mine and the house are pictured but not labeled by name on topographical maps. See Map # 4, Appendix D.)

*A hiker enjoys the view of Pinto Basin from the pass above Eldorado Mine*

## 6. ELDORADO MINE

**Type:** road-trail/x-country, day/overnight
**Mileage:** 7.5 miles to PR#11 (11 miles round trip to mine)
**Time:** 4 - 5 hours, (6 - 7 hours)
**Difficulty:** moderate
**Elevation Extremes:** 2360' (2600') - 3250 **Difference:** 880' (650')
**Starting Point:** Pleasant Valley Backcountry Board (3250')
**Ending Point:** Park Route #11, milepost 8 - 2560' or Pleasant Valley Backcountry Board
**Topo Maps:** Malapai Hill 7.5', Fried Liver Wash 7.5'

Summary: This is not the shortest route to Eldorado Mine (the route from PR#11 is shorter), but it is the most interesting. The route travels along Pleasant Valley, through the Hexie foothills to a picturesque pass which overlooks the Pinto Basin, then down Eldorado Wash to the mining ruins. The vegetation changes as the route descends from the Mojave Desert into the Colorado Desert. See Chapter 14, Hike # 4b for a description of Eldorado Mine. (The mine shafts are dangerous; maintain a safe distance from the openings. Refer to Chapter 3, "Hazards - Use Caution.")

Route: Follow the Pleasant Valley Road-Trail (page 59) to a small hill. (The road-trail enters a wash a short distance before the hill. Cross the wash to find the continuing road-trail.) Continue following the road-trail past a fence to a fork. Take the right fork. The road-trail is fairly easy to follow through the foothills, up to the pass, and part-way down the other side of the pass to a wash. When the road-trail becomes difficult to recognize, follow the wash the remaining distance to the mine and mining camp ruins. (To continue to Park Route #11, see Chapter 14, Hike # 4b, Eldorado Mine.)

## 7. FRIED LIVER WASH

**Type**: road-trail/x-country, day/overnight
**Mileage**: 14 miles (one-way)
**Time**: 7 - 9 hours
**Difficulty**: easy
**Elevation Extremes**: 1780' - 3250' **Difference:** 1470'
**Starting Point**: Pleasant Valley Backcountry Board (3250')
**Ending Point**: Fried Liver Wash - PR#11 (1780')
**Topo Maps**: Malapai Hill 7.5', Fried Liver Wash 7.5'

Summary: This route leads from Pleasant Valley to Pinto Basin via a wide, sandy wash that winds below high desert mountains. Vegetation along this route gradually changes as the hike travels from the Mojave Desert into the Colorado Desert. The wash provides a colorful spring wildflower display in the height of the flower season.

Route: Travel the Pleasant Valley Road-Trail (page 59) 2.5 miles to a sandy wash near the base of a small hill. Follow the wash (Fried Liver Wash) around the south side of the hill, through a mountain canyon, and down into Pinto Basin. When the wash exits the canyon into the open basin, it divides into several washes. Stay along the left wall of the canyon. Travel through the basin by taking the left of all major forks in the wash. This eventually leads to a large sandy wash which crosses Park Route #11. For vehicle shuttle purposes, the exit point onto Park Route #11 is located just west of the west-facing "Fried Liver Wash" sign (near mile 13). (Note: Flash flooding may periodically change the course of the wash. However, the wash will still cross Park Route #11 at some point near mile 13.)

## 8. BERNARD (5430') & LITTLE BERDOO (5440')

**Type**: x-country, day/overnight (note day use area on map)
**Mileage**: Route #1- 8.5 miles
Route #2- 6.5 miles via Nard Wash, Berdoo Canyon Road
11.5 miles via the backcountry board and Nard Wash
Mileage is to Little Berdoo. Subtract 1.5 miles round trip for Bernard Peak.
**Time**: 5 - 7 hours
**Difficulty**: strenuous, moderately difficult
**Elevation Extremes**: 3250' - 5440' **Difference:** 2190'
**Starting and Ending Point**: Stop #14 (3520'), Berdoo Canyon Road (3760'), or Pleasant Valley Backcountry Board (3250')
**Topo Maps**: Malapai Hill 7.5', Rockhouse Canyon 7.5'

Summary: Bernard Peak and Little Berdoo Peak are two adjacent mountains providing spectacular and different views. From Bernard there are views of the north valleys, Mt. San Jacinto and Mt. San Gorgonio. Little Berdoo provides sweeping views of the entire Coachella Valley. The hike to Bernard's summit is invigorating and picturesque. Little Berdoo's summit is attained by an additional, much easier, 3/4 mile hike from Bernard. A sheltered plateau between the two peaks provides pleasant flat areas for camping. There are climbing registers on both summits.

Route #1 North Wash: This is the easier of the two routes since it travels up the more gradual incline of the north wash. From Stop #14, backtrack 100 yards down the road (northeast) then walk easterly around the base of the mountains. Enter the first major wash and canyon. Follow the wash and take a left at the first fork in the wash. (In this next section of the wash, there will be a couple of low cliffs requiring class III-IV climbing.) One-half mile beyond the fork, the canyon opens up and the wash forks again. Take the left fork and head back into a narrow canyon. About 1/4 mile from this fork, the canyon again opens up and the wash widens. Continue in the wash past this point to reach a *perpendicular* wash junction on the right side. (There is another wash junction on the right side before this one, but it doesn't intersect the main wash at a 90° angle.) Leave the main wash and head SW up this side wash/gully. Follow this wash to a pass located a short distance below Bernard's summit. (Stay to the left in the narrow forks just below the pass.) From the pass, head SW up the ridge to the summit. The summit consists of two rock points with a long saddle between these points. The climbing register and benchmark are on the southern point. (See Map # 4, Appendix D.)

Route #2, Nard Wash: Although the route up Nard Wash is shorter, it is much steeper and more rugged than the route up the North Wash. Nard is an isolated peak located between the east base of Bernard Peak and the Berdoo Canyon Road. Nard Wash descends from Bernard, travels along the west base of Nard Peak, then heads north to the center of Pleasant Valley. The most direct access to Nard Wash is from a pull-out on the Berdoo Canyon Road, 1.8 miles south of the junction with Geology Tour Road. If the roads are dry, two-wheel drive vehicles can usually travel as far as this pullout. (For overnight trips, park at the backcountry board and hike up to the pullout either via the road or in the parallel wash.)

From the pullout, head SW about 250 yards to Nard Wash. Follow the wash south to the west side of Nard Peak; then head SW up the steep gully toward Bernard. Bernard, appearing as two peaks with a long saddle between, is the most distant peak above the gully. (There are two smaller rocky points in the center of the saddle.) Further up the gully, Bernard disappears and a new landmark becomes prominent; a point capped by a distinctive rocky knob rises above the gully. The summit can be gained by passing to either side of this point. Following the rocky wash up to the right of this point, and continuing to take the right of all above forks in the wash, leads to the pass described in Route #1. (See Map # 4, Appendix D.)

Little Berdoo Peak Route: From Bernard's summit, Little Berdoo can be seen to the southwest. It rises slightly higher than Bernard. Drop down the southwest slope of Bernard Peak and travel southwest up and over some small ridges. Cross a small plateau (good camping spot) and climb the slope to Little Berdoo Peak. The peak is marked by a tall stake with two square pieces of metal attached. (See Map # 4, Appendix D.)

# 9. PUSHAWALLA PLATEAU

**Type**: road-trail/x-country, day (note day use area on map)
**Mileage**: 6.5 miles
**Time**: 4 - 5 hours
**Difficulty**: moderately strenuous
**Elevation Extremes**: 3660' - 5200' **Difference:** 1540'
**Starting and Ending Point**: Pinyon Well Parking Area (3660')
**Topo Maps**: Malapai Hill 7.5'

Summary: This hike offers a variety of vegetation, historical sites, and great views in a quiet, seldom-visited part of the monument. Pinyon Well was the location of a major source of water during the mining days. A small community thrived near the well. The watering trough, water-holding tanks, wells, and building foundations that were a part of this community can be seen on the way to Pushawalla Plateau. Water still seeps from one well attracting birds and wildlife.

Just before the plateau, the road-trail passes the mine shafts and building ruins of the Pinyon Mine (also known as the Tingman-Holland Mine). This mine was among one of the first mines to be constructed in the monument area. The mine's shafts were lined with logs rather than milled planks and beams. (The mine shafts are dangerous; maintain a safe distance from their openings. Refer to Chapter 3, "Hazards - Use Caution.")

The road-trail continues past the Pinyon Mine to Pushawalla Plateau, the highlight of this hike. The spectacular view from Pushawalla Plateau includes the Coachella Valley from the Salton Sea to Palm Springs, as well as the monument valleys and mountains to the north.

A short side trip on this hike leads to another significant mining site, the Hensen Well mill site. The remains of four stone buildings and a fireplace chimney line the sides of the wash above the site of the mill. However, it is the Chilean mill and not the building structures which makes this site historically interesting. In the early 1900's, ore from many of the nearby mines was brought to this Chilean mill for custom grinding. Most milling arrastras of this era used drag stones to grind ore. The Chilean mill used large cement-filled cast iron wheels which rolled over and crushed the ore within the arrastra. Two of these massive crushing wheels can still be found on site.

Route: Follow the road-trail southwest from the parking area, through a canyon, to the site of Pinyon Well. Continue up the canyon to a fork (about 1.5 miles from the parking area). The right fork leads to a dead end. Take the left fork. About 1/3 mile beyond the fork, the wash/canyon turns south (left). ** Keep to the right and stay on the road-trail which is washed out and not very obvious. Continue following the road-trail uphill for another 0.3 miles. At this point, a rocky and steeper road-trail branches to the left and travels south.

Follow this southern road-trail uphill through the mountains. Sections of this road-trail are rough and steep but easy to follow. The road-trail fades out upon a broad scenic plateau dotted with small rocky peaks and vegetated with oaks, pinyon pines, Joshua trees, and yuccas. Note: Following the main road-trail 100 yards past the southbound junction leads to a pass and wire-cable fence. Continuing past the fence leads down through Pushawalla Canyon to the boundary and eventually out to Dillon Road in Desert Hot Springs. (See Map # 4, Appendix D.)

** Hensen Well: This side trip begins at the point where the road-trail departs the wash. From this junction, continue about 125 yards south in the wash. Exit right out of the main wash and follow a smaller sandy side wash. Follow this side wash up into a rocky gully. Climb a short ways up through the rocky gully to reach the ruins and mill site. To continue on the Pushawalla route, backtrack the 0.3 miles to the road-trail/wash junction. (Note: The ruins are marked on the 7.5' topographical map.)

*Pushawalla Plateau provides sweeping views of the Coachella Valley and Mt. San Jacinto*

# 10. BLUE CUT LOOP

**Type**: road-trail/x-country, day/overnight (note day use area on map)
**Mileage**: 14.5 miles
**Time**: 8-10 hours
**Difficulty**: moderately strenuous
**Elevation Extremes**: 2750' - 4620' **Difference:** 1870'
**Starting and Ending Point**: Pinyon Well Parking Area (3660')
**Topo Maps**: Malapai Hill 7.5', Keys View 7.5'

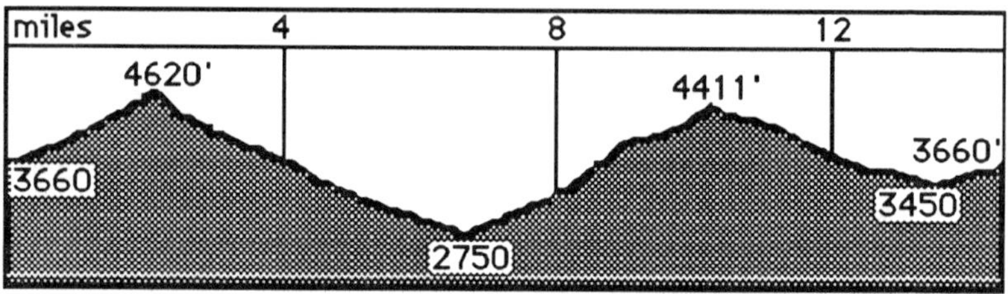


Summary: During the early mining days, the Blue Cut Wash was the original route of travel for mule team wagons. These teams travelled from the railroad depots in the low desert, over Blue Cut Pass, and on to mines in Pleasant Valley and in the Lost Horse Mountain area. In later years, another route, up and over Pushawalla Pass, was created to reach Pleasant Valley. Both routes have long since been closed to vehicle traffic and are well on their way to being reclaimed by nature. Although the Pushawalla Pass route is readily visible in many places, the Blue Cut Pass route is all but vanished. A discerning eye will be able to find the slight trace of a wagon trail at the top of Blue Cut Pass.

This hike takes in both of these early wagon trail routes. The hike provides a variety of views, terrain, and vegetation as it leads up and over the two passes. As the route ascends up through a canyon to Pushawalla Pass, it travels past the historical Pinyon Well site. (See Pushawalla Plateau, Hike # 9, for a description of Pinyon Well.) At the pass, take in the excellent views of Mt. San Jacinto before heading down into Pushawalla Canyon and into the low desert.

At the lowest portion of the hike, near the bottom of Blue Cut Wash, spring wildflowers are sometimes abundant. Watch the vegetation change along the way as the Blue Cut Wash gradually leads from the low Colorado Desert back up to the Mojave Desert. A thriving group of large Joshua trees, the most notable plant of the Mojave Desert, grows on the broad flat area of Blue Cut Pass.

This trip should be planned either as an overnight trip or a very long day trip. The 1870' difference in elevation extremes, the continual up and down travel, and soft sand contribute to slow travel.

Route: The recommended direction of travel is clockwise. This puts the higher of the two pass climbs at the beginning of the trip and allows for easy downhill travel over the softer, sandier portion of the trip. Follow the road-trail southwest from the parking area, through a canyon, to the site of Pinyon Well. Continue up the canyon to a fork (about 1.5 miles from the parking area). The right fork leads to a dead end. Take the left fork. About 1/3 mile beyond the fork, the wash/canyon turns south (left). Keep to the right and stay on the road-trail which is washed out and not very obvious. Continue following the road-trail uphill to Pushawalla Pass. (A wire/cable fence is located at the pass.)

From Pushawalla Pass, travel down the road-trail and wash 3.5 miles to an area where the canyon opens up. At this point, there is a broad open basin on the right side of the wash and a large side wash and valley located on the left. Mt. San Jacinto looms above the main wash. Continue 1.25 miles through the open area and back down into a canyon to reach the junction with Blue Cut Wash. The Blue Cut Wash is a major wash; however, it's size is not readily obvious at the junction. (It would be easy to miss this turn.) The mouth of the Blue Cut Wash is about 30-40' in width. A 20' high cliff is located on either side of the wash entrance.

Travel up Blue Cut Wash through a short canyon. There are several small side washes; stay in main wash. The main wash forks a couple times within the first 1/2 mile; take the right forks. The canyon eventually opens up into a basin. Continue following the wash through the basin and up into Blue Cut Canyon. Within the canyon, there is a major wash/side valley which descends from the left. Do not turn left into this large side canyon; continue straight into the narrow canyon. Continue 1.5 miles to Blue Cut Pass. Near the top of the pass, the wash forks; take the right or straighter fork. Cross the pass and follow a wash down into Pleasant Valley. Travel southeast around the base of mountains and back to the Geology Tour Road and the parking area. (See Map # 4, Appendix D.)

# Chapter 10

# KEYS VIEW ROAD (PR#13)

Keys View Road begins from Park Route #12, 14.8 miles from the North Entrance and 10.5 miles from the West Entrance. The five-mile road travels through the high Mojave Desert from Cap Rock to Keys View. This road is a starting point for many excellent hikes to high peaks, good viewpoints, historical landmarks and prime wildlife habitat areas. The Juniper Flats Backcountry Board is located on the west side of the Keys View Road about one mile from Cap Rock. Nearby campgrounds include Hidden Valley, 1.7 miles west on Park Route #12; and Ryan, 0.5 miles east on Park Route #12.

## 1. CAP ROCK NATURE TRAIL - (See Chapter 5, Hike # 4.)

## 2. JUNIPER FLATS

**Type:** trail, day/ overnight (note day use area on map)
**Mileage:** 9 miles
**Time:** 4 - 6 hours
**Difficulty:** easy
**Elevation Extremes:** 4340' - 4840' **Difference:** 500'
**Starting and Ending Point:** Juniper Flats Backcountry Board (4340')
**Topo Maps:** Keys View 7.5'

Summary: Juniper Flats is an extensive, relatively level area thickly vegetated with large juniper trees. The area can be reached either via the Riding and Hiking Trail or a dirt road (closed to vehicles), both of which leave from the backcountry board. The trail, which is slightly shorter than the road, provides better views and more interesting terrain. Halfway to the flats, the trail follows along a ridge offering excellent views of the Wonderland. Farther up the trail, there are good views of Mt. San Jacinto. Watch for wildlife along the way. Juniper Flats and Quail Mountain are both favorite areas for the mule deer which inhabit the monument.

The trail crosses the dirt road 4.5 miles from the trailhead. The road continues to the north another 1/2 mile. Continuing on the trail leads to

Covington Flats (see Chapter 11, Hike # 2). There are many excellent camping spots throughout Juniper Flats (note day use areas). (See Map # 5, Appendix D.)

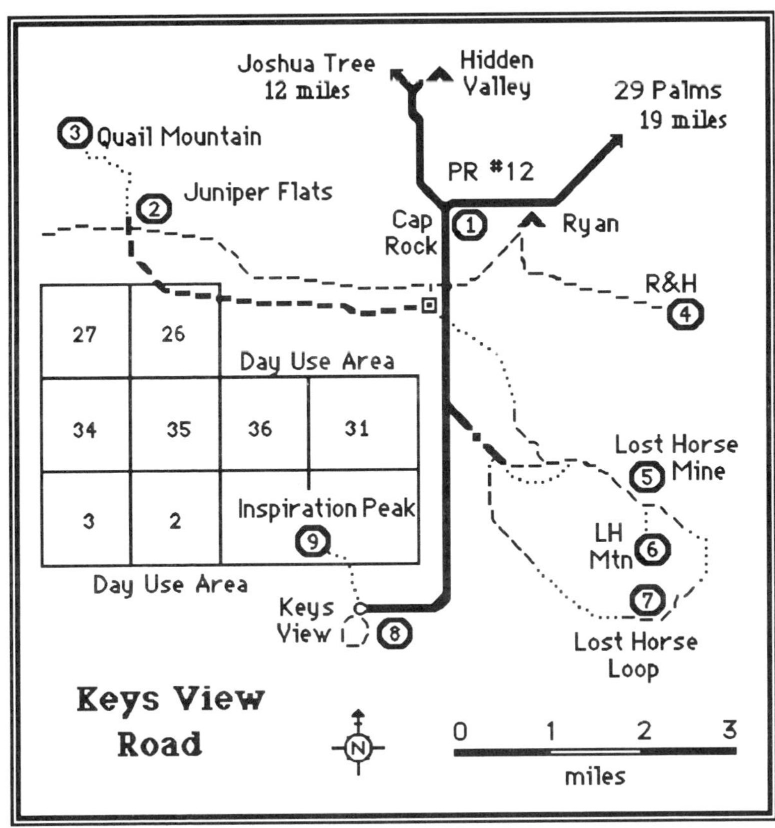


## 3. QUAIL MOUNTAIN (5813')

**Type:** trail/x-country, day/overnight
**Mileage:** 12 miles
**Time:** 6 - 8 hours
**Difficulty:** strenuous
**Elevation Extremes:** 4340' - 5813' **Difference:** 1473'
**Starting and Ending Point:** Juniper Flats Backcountry Board (4340')
**Topo Maps:** Keys View 7.5', Indian Cove 7.5'

Summary: A relatively straightforward route leads to the top of the highest peak in the monument. The ascent is either up the mountain's southeast ridge or up the southeast wash. The wash is more picturesque;

it travels up through a narrow, sandy-floored canyon lined with large yuccas, nolinas, and pines. Much of the vegetation on the upper portion of the mountain is dead and fire-scarred from a large wildland fire that occurred in 1978.

On a clear day, the 360° view from the summit is outstanding. The Salton Sea, Mt. San Gorgonio, Mt. San Jacinto, Wonderland of Rocks, Lost Horse Valley and nearby small desert towns are all part of the panorama. Deer are frequently sighted near the top of the mountain. A climbing register is located on the summit.

Route: Travel the dirt road or trail to Juniper Flats (see preceding hike). From the end of the road, head NNW (approximately 3/4 mile) to either the southeast ridge or to the wash just below and west of the ridge. To travel the wash route, hike up the wash to a fork. Follow the right fork up to a ridge located just east of the summit. Travel west up the ridge to the summit which is marked by a large cairn.

## 4. CALIFORNIA RIDING & HIKING TRAIL

(See Chapter 11)

*Joshua trees frame Mt. San Jacinto at Juniper Flats*

*Lost Horse Mine Stamp Mill*

## 5. LOST HORSE MINE

**Type:** trail, day
**Mileage:** 4 miles
**Time:** 2 - 3 hours
**Difficulty:** moderate
**Elevation Extremes:** 4600' - 5080' (5188') **Difference:** 480' (588')
**Starting and Ending Point:** Lost Horse Mine Parking Area (4600')
**Topo Maps:** Keys View 7.5'

Summary: The Lost Horse Mine operation was one of the most successful mining operations within the monument. Today the building structures of this mine are the best preserved of any mine complex within the National Park System. Many of the structures that were once a part of this extensive operation have been leveled; however, the significant remains of the ten-stamp mill are still standing. Several large cyanide settling tanks, stone building foundations, and miscellaneous mining equipment surround the mill. Most of the mine shafts have been fenced or sealed. (Mine shafts are dangerous; maintain a safe distance from their openings.) A lack of Joshua trees may be noted around the mine area. The trees which were used for fuel during the mining days have yet to regenerate.

The trail to the mine, which is actually the old mining road, gradually winds up through rolling hills. Take the additional short, steep hike

(NE) to the top of the hill (5188') behind the stamp mill. The hilltop offers good views of Pleasant Valley, Pinto Basin, Mt. San Gorgonio, Mt. San Jacinto, Lost Horse Valley, and the Wonderland of Rocks.

Alternative Route: This route leaves from the parking area, travels up through a sandy wash, and joins the Lost Horse Mine trail about one mile before the mine. The steep-sided wash lined with pines and nolinas provides pleasant hiking and a variety of vegetation. Shade offered by the pines is welcomed on a warm day.

Follow the wash ENE from the parking area. Stay in the main sandy wash rather than traveling up any of the rocky side washes. When the wash fades out, head NE 50 yards to the main trail. Travel the trail (right) the remaining distance to the mine. (See Map # 5, Appendix D.)

*Lost Horse Mountain offers excellent views of Pleasant Valley and Malapai Hill*

## 6. LOST HORSE MOUNTAIN (5313')

**Type:** trail/x-country, day
**Mileage:** 4.5 miles
**Time:** 3 hours
**Difficulty:** moderately strenuous
**Elevation Extremes:** 4600' - 5313' **Difference:** 713'
**Starting and Ending Point:** Lost Horse Mine Parking Area (4600')
**Topo Maps:** Keys View 7.5'

Summary: Lost Horse Mountain is one of the easier mountains to climb within the monument. An additional 1/4 mile hike leads from Lost Horse Mine to the summit of Lost Horse Mountain. The peak offers spectacular views of Pleasant Valley, Mt. San Gorgonio, Mt. San Jacinto, Lost Horse and Queen valleys, the Wonderland of Rocks, and part of the Pinto Basin. There is a climbing register on the summit.

Route: From Lost Horse Mine (preceding hike), follow the road-trail SE to a pass located a short distance beyond the mine area. From here head SSW (right) up the slope to the summit saddle. The summit is the furthest point to the SE. (See Map # 5, Appendix D.)

## 7. LOST HORSE LOOP

**Type:** road-trail/x-country, day/ overnight
**Mileage:** 8.4 miles
**Time:** 5 - 6 hours
**Difficulty:** moderately strenuous
**Elevation Extremes:** 4600' - 5120' **Difference:** 520'
**Starting and Ending Point:** Lost Horse Mine Parking Area (4600')
**Topo Maps:** Keys View 7.5'

Summary: This is a good hike for those who would like to make the trip to Lost Horse Mine longer and more adventuresome. During the mining days, this loop was a complete circle of road and trail. Nature has since reclaimed many parts of the loop, making this a partial x-country route. The route travels along and then over a high ridge to a remote valley where the mine shafts and camp ruins of the Optimist Mine are located. (The mine shafts are dangerous, especially the vertical shaft. Maintain a safe distance from the shaft openings. Refer to Chapter 3, "Hazards-Use Caution.")

The south side of the loop provides remote, pleasant places to camp among Joshua trees and pinyon pines. A short side trip leads to the site of a Joshua tree log house -- part of the Gold Standard Mine operation. All that remains of the house is a wall of logs about two feet high. (Note for backpackers: See below, "Starting from Juniper Flats Back-country Board.")

Route: From Lost Horse Mine (see page 71), continue following the road-trail SE up and over a pass. Travel down a rough, steep road-trail to another mine (Lang Mine). Follow an obscure foot trail which begins directly on the other side of this mine. The foot trail fades out after approximately 1/4 mile. From this point, travel SW to the ridgetop where mine tailings (Optimist Mine), a fireplace chimney, and a road-trail can be seen on the other side. Descend to the road-trail and follow it through rolling hills to a wash.

Pleasant camping areas can be found at this road-trail/wash junction or southeast up the wash. The Joshua tree house can be found 1/4 mile (southeast) up the wash. Complete the loop by traveling NW either in the wash or on the road-trail. (The road-trail is difficult to follow.) Both wash and road-trail exit onto the main dirt road at approximately the same location. A right turn on this road leads to the parking lot (200 yards away).

Starting from Juniper Flats Backcountry Board: Cross Keys View Road and head SE past the southern end of the nearest roadside hill. Continue SE to a wash/gully that runs north-south between the mountains. Follow the wash south. A road-trail leaves the wash on the right side and leads to the Lost Horse Mine trail. The two trails join approximately 1/4 mile east of the Lost Horse Mine Parking Area. It is two miles from the backcountry board to the Lost Horse Mine trail. (See Map # 5, Appendix D.)

## 8. KEYS VIEW LOOP - (See Chapter 5, Hike # 5.)

## 9. INSPIRATION PEAK (5558')

**Type:** trail, day
**Mileage:** 1.5 miles
**Time:** 1 - 1.5 hours
**Difficulty:** moderately strenuous
**Elevation Extremes:** 5150' - 5558' **Difference:** 408'
**Starting and Ending Point:** Keys View (5150')
**Topo Maps:** Keys View 7.5'

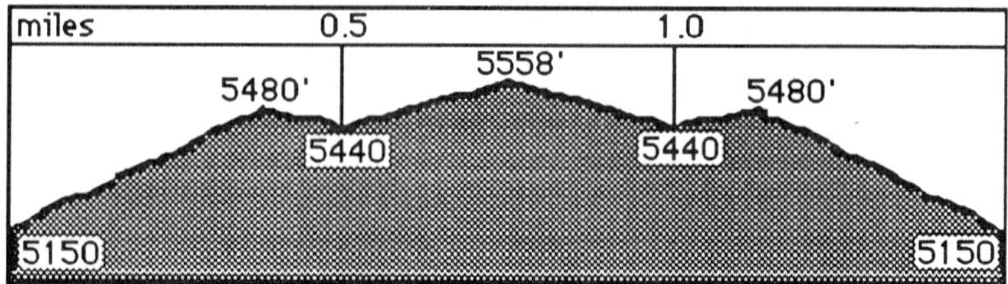

Summary: Inspiration Peak lies a short distance from Keys View on the crest of the Little San Bernardino Mountains. Keys View is well known for its spectacular view of the Coachella Valley, Mt. San Jacinto, Mt. San Gorgonio, and the Salton Sea. The panoramic view from Inspiration Peak is even more impressive and more encompassing. The circular vista includes a more extensive view of the Coachella Valley and the Salton Sea, as well as splendid views of the monument interior -- the Wonderland, Queen and Lost Horse valleys, and part of the Pinto Basin.

The trail starts at the NW side of the parking lot. It travels up and along a broad high point, descends to a saddle, then continues up to the actual summit. There are good views obtained from the first high point. However, the best views are obtained from the summit of the impressive, steep faced peak at the end of the trail. The trail actually stops just short of the summit. From the trail's end, scramble the remaining 30' up over a rock pile to reach the top of the peak. (See Map # 5, Appendix D.)

*Keys View*

# Chapter 11

# CALIFORNIA RIDING AND HIKING TRAIL

Thirty-five miles of the California Riding and Hiking Trail traverse the monument from Black Rock, in the western-most part of the monument, to the North Entrance near Twentynine Palms. As the trail travels from west to east, it passes through areas having distinct vegetation differences -- from the upper pinyon/juniper forests, through Joshua tree forests, to lower elevations where creosote is the predominant vegetation. The trail can be hiked either in its entirety, which takes two to three days, or in shorter sections of 4.4 to 10 miles. In general, it is easier to travel from west to east since the western sections of the trail are at higher elevations.

## 1. BLACK ROCK TO COVINGTON FLATS

**Type**: trail/x-country, day/overnight
**Mileage**: 7.5 miles
**Time**: 3 - 5 hours
**Difficulty**: moderate
**Elevation Extremes**: 3940' - 5120' **Difference:** 1180'
**Starting Point**: Black Rock Trailhead (3980')
**Ending Point**: Covington Flats Backcountry Board (4820')
**Topo Maps**: Yucca Valley South 7.5', Joshua Tree South 7.5'

Summary: The trail leads gradually uphill from Black Rock to Covington. (This is one segment of the Riding and Hiking Trail that would be easier traveled from east to west.) The first section of the trail passes through hills overlooking Yucca Valley. This area is vegetated with pinyon pines, junipers, and Joshua trees. The middle section of the hike, which is on a blazed route rather than a trail, travels up a sandy wash bordered by large hills. The last section of the hike follows the Upper Covington Flats Road.

Route: Follow the trail/route marked with white posts. The blazed trail/route leads to the Upper Covington Flats Road. From here, follow the road SE two miles to the backcountry board parking area. Carrying a map and compass is advised just in case the trail posts are missing. (See Map # 1 & 7, Appendix D.)

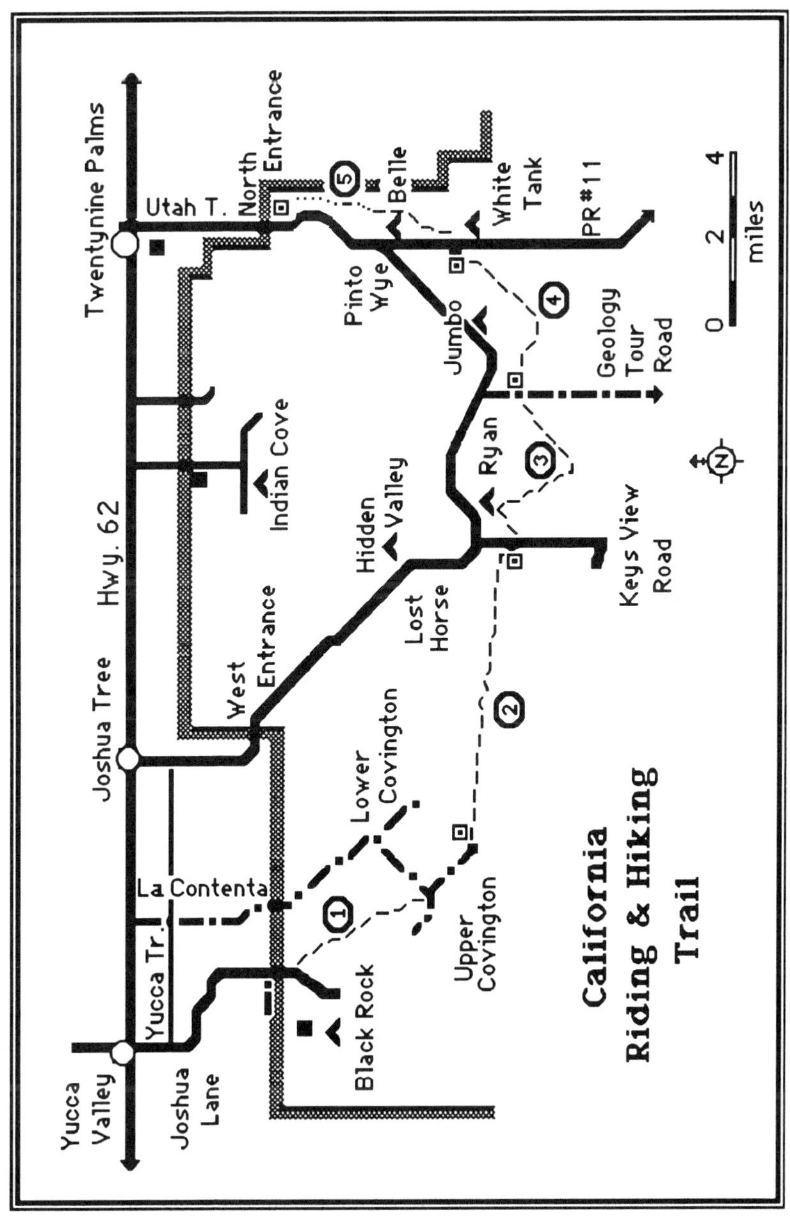

## 2. COVINGTON FLATS TO KEYS VIEW ROAD

**Type:** trail, day/overnight
**Mileage**: 10 miles
**Time:** 5 - 7 hours
**Difficulty:** moderately strenuous
**Elevation Extremes:** 4160' - 5000' **Difference:** 840'
**Starting Point**: Covington Flats Backcountry Board (4820')
**Ending Point**: Juniper Flats Backcountry Board (4340')
**Topo Maps:** Joshua Tree South 7.5', East Deception Canyon 7.5', Keys View 7.5'

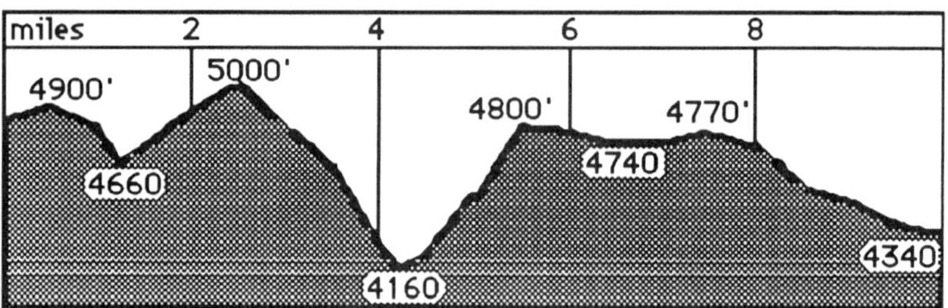


Summary: Of the five Riding & Hiking Trail sections, this section has the greatest variety of terrain, vegetation, and scenic views. The largest known Joshua tree in the monument is located 0.2 miles from the trailhead. The tree stands about thirty-five feet high and has a circumference of about seventeen feet at the base. The trail travels past this tree and through more large Joshua trees.

Farther on, the trail winds around a hillside through thicker vegetation -- juniper, pinyon pine, and jojoba. A few switchbacks lead down the hillside to a flat valley, an excellent place for overnight camping (two miles from the Covington Trailhead). Distant Mt. San Gorgonio rises above this picturesque valley.

The trail continues up out of the valley to a plateau then travels along a high ridge. From the ridge, the view of the Salton Sea is excellent. A rocky, somewhat rough trail descends the ridge, travels along a lower hillside, then zigzags up to Juniper Flats. Tracks and droppings indicate that the elusive bighorn sheep frequent this area. The remaining 4.5 miles of the trail move gradually downhill to Keys View Road. (See Chapter 10, Hike # 2, Juniper Flats.)

## 3. KEYS VIEW ROAD TO GEOLOGY TOUR ROAD

**Type:** trail, day/overnight
**Mileage:** 6.5 miles
**Time:** 3 - 4 hours
**Difficulty:** easy
**Elevation Extremes:** 4340' - 4540' **Difference:** 200'
**Starting Point:** Juniper Flats Backcountry Board (4340')
**Ending Point:** Geology Tour Road Backcountry Board (4493')
**Topo Maps:** Keys view 7.5', Malapai Hill 7.5'

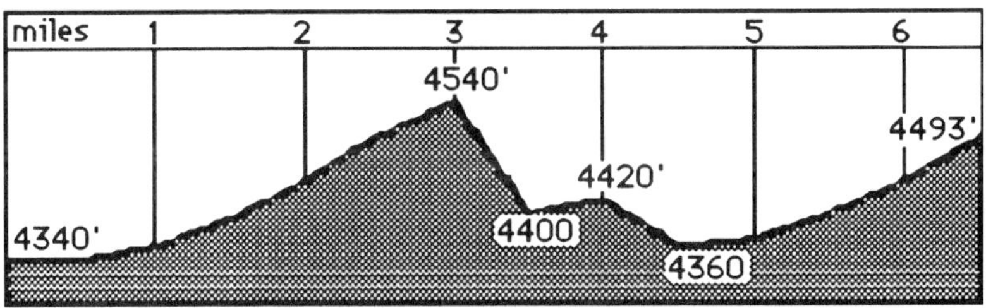


Summary: This trail travels from Lost Horse Valley to Queen Valley via a low pass between Ryan and Lost Horse mountains. The two-mile section of trail that travels between the mountains gradually leads up to the pass then gradually down the other side of the pass into Queen Valley. East of the pass, the trail passes a horizontal mine shaft (unsafe for entry) located thirty feet to the right of the trail. A short distance beyond the mine and on the opposite side of the trail, there are remains of a camp where a prospector once stayed.

This is just one of the many mining camp ruins that can be found throughout the monument. A few lucky and industrious desert pioneers did discover rich deposits of gold as is evidenced by the success of the Lost Horse and Desert Queen Mines. However, the majority of the pioneer prospectors were hardly able to scrape out a meager existence. Ruins, such as this one, are all that remain of unfulfilled dreams of gold and great wealth.

The trail can also be accessed from Ryan Campground; this shortens the hike by 3/4 mile. For overnight trips, vehicles should be parked at the backcountry board rather than at Ryan Campground. (See Map # 5, Appendix D.)

## 4. GEOLOGY TOUR ROAD TO PARK ROUTE #11

**Type**: trail, day/ overnight
**Mileage**: 4.4 miles
**Time**: 2 - 3 hours
**Difficulty**: easy
**Elevation Extremes**: 3900'- 4493' **Difference:** 593'
**Starting Point**: Geology Tour Road Backcountry Board (4493')
**Ending Point**: Twin Tanks Backcountry Board (3900')
**Topo Maps**: Malapai Hill 7.5'

Summary: This is the shortest and easiest section of the Riding & Hiking Trail. It travels gradually downhill as it leads from west to east across Queen Valley. Approximately two miles from Geology Tour Road, the trail passes near large rock formations. These rock formations provide a scenic and sheltered place to camp or have lunch. The remainder of the hike travels through the open valley where there are good views down into Pinto Basin and beyond to the distant Coxcomb Mountains. (See Map # 2 Appendix D.)

## 5. PARK ROUTE #11 TO NORTH ENTRANCE

**Type**: trail/x-country, day/overnight
**Mileage:** 7 miles
**Time:** 3 - 4 hours
**Difficulty**: easy
**Elevation Extremes**: 2880' - 3900' **Difference:** 1020'
**Starting Point**: Twin Tanks Backcountry Board (3900')
**Ending Point**: North Entrance Backcountry Board (2880')
**Topo Maps**: Malapai Hill 7.5', Queen Mtn. 7.5'

Summary: The final section of the Riding & Hiking Trail is the least maintained. The majority of the trail has become overgrown and washed out. A topographical map is essential if staying on the trail is desired. The trail/ route parallels the road its entire length, although it is far enough removed from the road to obscure the sound of motors. The most interesting section of the trail is the first three miles near the Twin Tanks Backcountry Board. This section travels along the base of Belle Mountain and through rock piles east of Belle Campground. The terrain and views along the trail north of Pinto Wye is similar to the terrain and views along the roadway. (See Map # 2, Appendix D.)

# Chapter 12

# INDIAN COVE / FORTYNINE PALMS

The Indian Cove / Fortynine Palms area is located along the northern edge of the monument. The area is popular during the cooler months of the year, since the area is generally warmer and more sheltered than the higher sections of the monument. Two roads lead to this area off Hwy 62 -- Indian Cove Road and Canyon Road. Indian Cove Road (located 5.7 miles west of Adobe Road in Twentynine Palms and 9 miles east of Park Boulevard in Joshua Tree) leads to a ranger station, picnic area, and a 110 site campground. Hikes leaving from Indian Cove lead into the Wonderland of Rocks or skirt around the Wonderland through gentler terrain. The Indian Cove Backcountry Board is on the west side of the road, 1/2 mile south of the ranger station. Canyon Road is located 1.7 miles east of Indian Cove Road. The trail at the road's end leads to a beautiful oasis and a wild, rocky canyon. (See map on page 82.)

## 1. BOY SCOUT TRAIL - (See Chapter 7, Hike # 5.)

## 2. INDIAN COVE NATURE TRAIL

(See Chapter 5, Hike # 7.)

## 3. GUN SIGHT LOOP

**Type**: x-country, day
**Mileage**: 2.75 mile loop
**Time**: 4 hours
**Difficulty**: strenuous, difficult (+)
**Elevation Extremes**: 3300' - 4100' **Difference**: 800'
**Starting and Ending Point**: Indian Cove Campground, west end (3334')
**Topo Map:** Indian Cove 7.5'

Summary: This is an adventuresome hike which covers some beautiful, but extremely rugged terrain. The route travels 800' up a steep draw filled with slick rock canyons and boulder caves. The route is not recommended for anyone less than proficient in serious boulder scrambling.

Following the ascent, the route travels through a high, relatively level, rock-enclosed valley, then descends another draw which is nearly as rugged as the first.

In the upper valley, the route passes beneath a cave located about 100' above the wash in a rock formation. The cave, which is now empty, may have been used by early Indian tribes which roamed through this area on hunting and food gathering expeditions. These ancient people often used rock overhangs and caves for temporary shelter and storage. (The climb up into the cave is treacherous and not recommended.)

From the descent route, there are periodic views out beyond the rocky maze of the Wonderland into the gentler desert which houses local communities. In the last 3/4 mile of the hike, the terrain flattens out. The wash is wider, filled with sand, and forested with short willows.

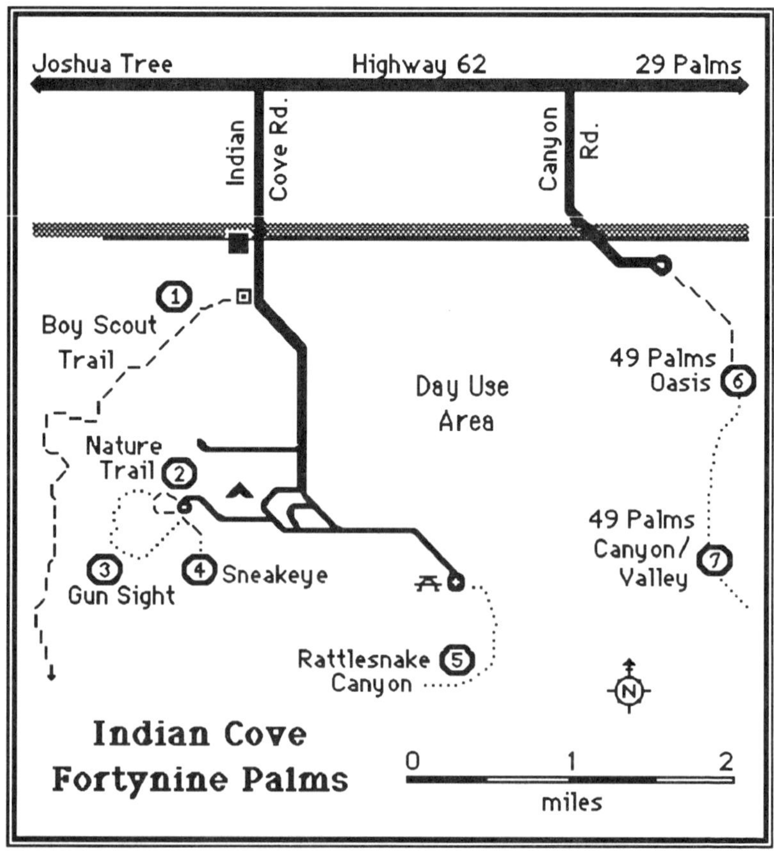

Route: Park at the end of the loop at the west end of the campground. Look SW toward the obvious low notch known as the "Gun Sight." The route travels up through the boulder filled canyon, Gun Sight Canyon, to the top of this notch. (The climb is every bit as difficult as it looks.)

From the parking lot, follow the road-trail southwest about 100 yards. Depart the road-trail and continue southwest to the base of Gun Sight Canyon. Scramble up the canyon. About 3/4 mile from the base, the canyon opens up into a small valley. Travel a short ways up the wash to a fork. Take the right fork. Continue traveling 1/2 mile up the wash which tops out in a gentle, high valley. Travel around the rock formations to the right over relatively level ground.

A wash will soon begin a gentle descent to the north. The gentleness is short lived. Travel again becomes extreme as the wash descends nearly 600' in about 1/4 mile. At the bottom of the steep descent, follow the now gentle wash down through the willow trees to the intersection with the nature trail wash. Turn right at the wash junction and travel about 100' up the wash to the nature trail signs. Follow the nature trail east back to the parking lot. (See Map # 6, Appendix D.)

## 4. SNEAKEYE SPRING

**Type**: road-trail/x-country, day
**Mileage**: 1 mile
**Time**: 1 hour
**Difficulty**: moderate, difficult
**Elevation Extremes**: 3334' - 3500' **Difference**: 166'
**Starting and Ending Point**: Indian Cove Campground, west end (3334')
**Topo Map:** Indian Cove 7.5'

Summary: Prior to the 1940's, Sneakeye Spring was a productive water source. Today, the only water found in the area is rainwater caught in the series of granite slab potholes which surround the spring site. However, some man-made remains of a water collection system indicate the spring was not always dry.

These remains include a couple of low cement walls (tanks) with a valve protruding from one of the cement walls. In addition, there is a rock and cement tank in the wash at the base of the draw. Undoubtedly, it was used to collect the piped spring water. According to local legend, this water collection system was used by bootleggers during the prohibition days. A traveling freight man known as Iron Wheel Johnson picked up the illegal booze and brought it down to the cities to sell.

The hike to Sneakeye Spring is short but a little challenging. It involves scrambling up through a rocky draw filled with large boulders. The spring site and the remains of the water collection system are located in a small, but relatively flat, open area vegetated with scrub oak trees. Travel beyond the spring site becomes more difficult.

Route: Park at the end of the loop at the west end of the campground. Follow the road-trail which leads southwest from the parking lot, curves around a rock formation, then heads southeast. The road-trail follows along a ridgetop and leads to the end of a ridge. From here, a narrower trail leads down and south about 50' to a high point above the wash. Sneakeye is located (S) up in the rocky draw on the other side of the wash.

Continue on a footpath SSW down the ridge to the bottom of the wash. (The rock and cement still tank is located under an oak tree in the wash bottom about 25' west of the rocky draw.) Cross the wash and scramble up the draw about 100 vertical feet. Follow a shallow slick-rock slot canyon which curves around to the right and leads to the open area vegetated with oaks. (See Map # 6, Appendix D.)

## 5. RATTLESNAKE CANYON

**Type**: x-country, day
**Mileage**: 3 miles
**Time**: 3 hours
**Difficulty**: strenuous, difficult
**Elevation Extremes**: 3017' - 3400' **Difference:** 383'
**Starting and Ending Point**: Indian Cove Picnic Area (3017')
**Topo Maps**: Indian Cove 7.5'

Summary: The highlight of Rattlesnake Canyon is a polished slot canyon located 0.4 miles up the wash from the picnic area. After rainstorms, water swirls in large potholes as it cascades down through the multi-leveled canyon. Some of these potholes retain water throughout much of the year. For many hikers, the slot canyon and adjacent smooth slab are a natural barrier to further travel. Those adventurous few who continue to the upper reaches of Rattlesnake Canyon discover a lovely sandy wash set between steep, rocky walls. Cottonwoods and other leafy deciduous trees brighten this isolated upper canyon and provide seasonal shade. (Rattlesnake Canyon is prone to flash floods. Refer to Chapter 3, Hazards - Use Caution.)

Route: Head east from the picnic area to a large wash and proceed south up the wash. The wash soon becomes cluttered with boulders. Some moderate boulder scrambling is necessary in order to reach the base of the slot canyon. Don't mistake a rocky alcove, which also has several large potholes, for the slot canyon. The slot canyon is just above the alcove. Climb out of the alcove along the left side. The easiest route around the slot canyon is to the right of the slot canyon and an adjacent slab (streaked with black desert varnish). Travel up along the right edge of the slab and under a large, left-pointing boulder. Continue up the rocky slope approximately 50 yards to a narrow gap in the rocks.

Traveling through the gap, which is partially hidden by two oak trees, leads to the top of the slot canyon. More scrambling above the slot canyon is necessary to reach the upper sandy wash. (See Map # 6, Appendix D.)

*Giant nolinas dwarf a hiker in a canyon above Indian Cove*

## 6. FORTYNINE PALMS OASIS

**Type**: trail, day
**Mileage**: 3 miles
**Time**: 2 - 3 hours
**Difficulty**: moderately strenuous
**Elevation Extremes**: 2720' - 3080' **Difference:** 360'
**Starting and Ending Point**: end of Canyon Road (2720')
**Topo Maps**: Queen Mtn. 7.5'

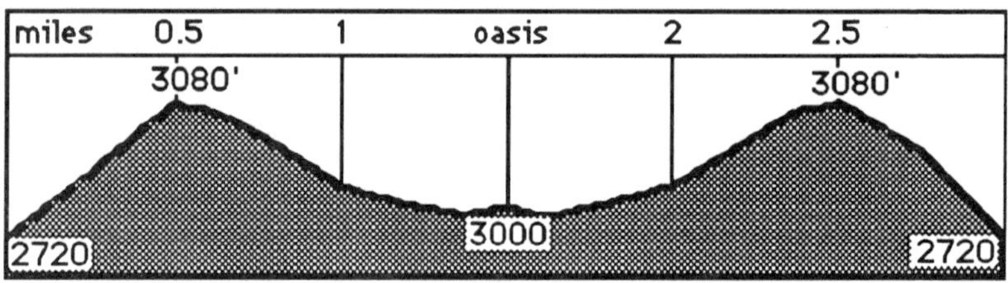


Summary: Fortynine Palms Oasis is one of five oases found within the monument. The well-maintained trail to this oasis ascends to a ridge above the parking lot. A concentrated display of barrel cacti can be found along the top of the ridge. The thick red spines and the large, round shape of the plant itself make this cactus easy to identify. After winding around the ridgetop, the trail steeply descends the other side of the ridge to the oasis.

The oasis is located in a rocky canyon where over fifty native fan palms tower above clear pools of water lined with emerald-green algae. Under the oasis canopy, there are large polished boulders which provide a place to rest and enjoy the natural life and sounds of this miniature ecosystem.

The palm trees at Fortynine Palms Oasis look noticeably different from the trees at the other oases in the monument. The trunks of many of the trees are black, and the characteristic skirts of dead palm fronds are absent. This is the result of four fires that have swept through the area since 1940. The black palm trunks supporting a bright green canopy give this oasis a unique beauty. (See Map # 6, Appendix D.)

## 7. FORTYNINE PALMS CANYON / VALLEY

**Type**: trail/x-country, day
**Mileage**: 6 miles round trip to beginning of valley
10 miles round trip to end of valley
**Time**: 6 - 9 hours
**Difficulty:** strenuous, difficult (+)
**Elevation Extremes**: 2720' - 4150' **Difference:** 1430'
**Starting and Ending Point**: end of Canyon Road (2720')
**Topo Maps**: Queen Mtn. 7.5'

Summary: This route quickly gains elevation as it ascends through a rugged, narrow canyon above Fortynine Palms Oasis. Eventually the walls of the canyon open to a high, picturesque valley where the coyote and the elusive desert bighorn find an isolated retreat. This hike should only be attempted by those confident in boulder scrambling. Having technical rock climbing skills and equipment is also suggested due to a couple of slick rock cliffs that bar the wash. The highest cliff, which has a rocky landing below, is 15-20' high.

Route: Hike the trail from the parking lot to Fortynine Palms Oasis (see preceding hike). From the oasis, travel south up the canyon. A spring, more palms, and a collection of willows are located in the wash 1/2 mile above the oasis. Beyond the spring, the canyon narrows and boulder scrambling becomes more difficult. The canyon exits into a small open area. Continue past the open area by traveling in the narrow canyon to the left. Emerge from the canyon into a long, wide valley. The center of this broad valley is dotted with small rocky hills. To reach the end of the valley, follow the wash along the northeast edge of these hills. (See Map # 6, Appendix D.)

# Chapter 13

# BLACK ROCK / COVINGTON FLATS

The Black Rock / Covington Flats area lies within the most western portion of the monument. It is an area of high elevation where some of the largest Joshua trees grow in dense concentrations. The area can be accessed from two locations. Joshua Lane in Yucca Valley leads to Black Rock Visitor Center, Ranger Station, and Campground (a 100 site campground with running water and flush toilets). Black Rock is the start of the California Riding and Hiking Trail. Other hikes from Black Rock include routes to high peaks with excellent views and routes along sandy washes that wind through picturesque canyons.

The second access to this area is on La Contenta Road which heads south off of Highway 62 in Yucca Valley. La Contenta leads to a system of dirt roads which travel through Covington Flats. Hikes from this area lead to Black Rock, travel down a lush canyon, or continue east through isolated mountains and valleys. A backcountry board is located at the east end of Upper Covington Flats. Backpackers may also register at Black Rock Ranger Station. Facilities at Black Rock may be closed during some months of the year. During these closures, the area usually remains open to hiking.

## 1. HIGH VIEW NATURE TRAIL - (See Chapter 5, Hike # 1.)

## 2. SOUTH PARK PEAK (4395')

**Type**: trail, day
**Mileage**: 0.8 mile loop
**Time:** 1 hour
**Difficulty**: moderate
**Elevation Extremes**: 4140' - 4395' **Difference:** 255'
**Starting and Ending Point**: South Park Parking Area (4140')
**Topo Maps**: Yucca Valley South 7.5'

Summary: This short loop trail is actually located just outside the monument. However, its closeness to Black Rock Campground makes it worthy of inclusion in this book. The trail is managed by the Yucca Valley Parks District.

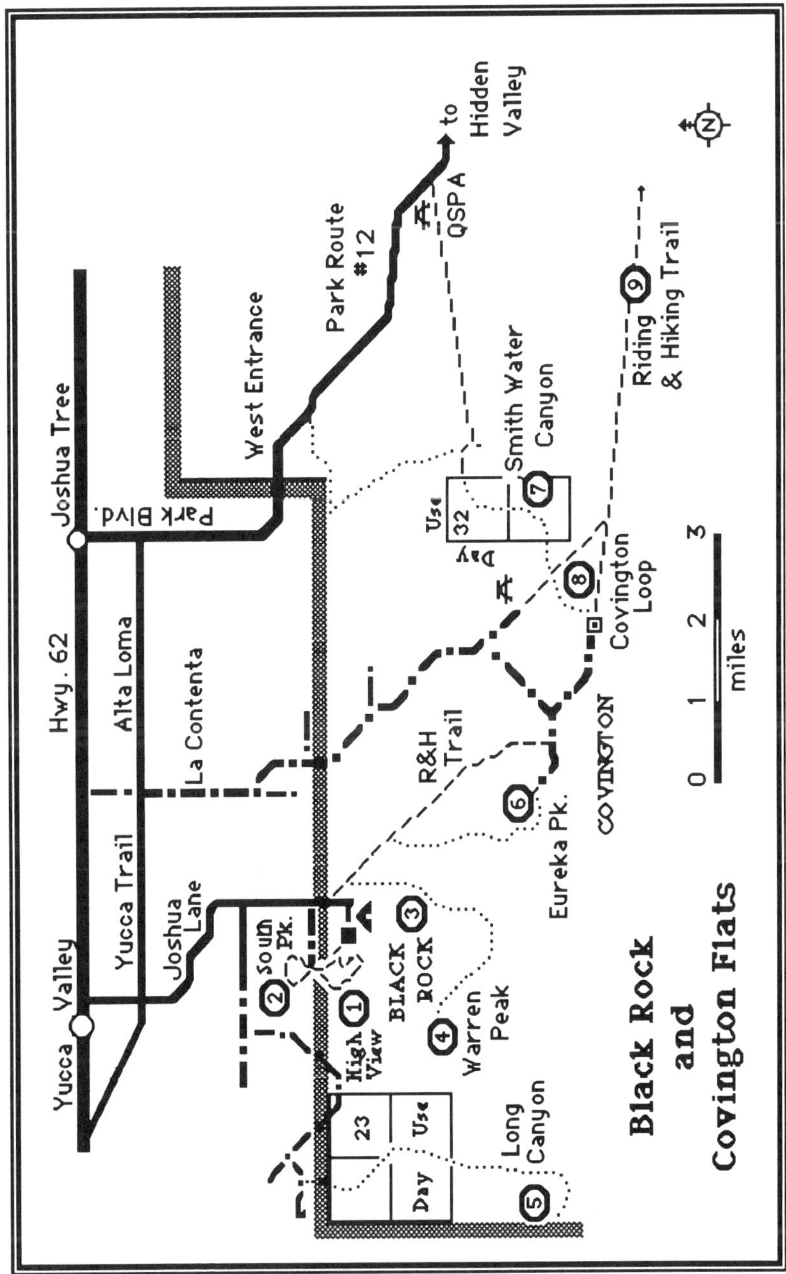


The trail leads a short distance up to the top of a peak which sits on the edge of the Morongo Basin. From the summit, there are unobstructed views of the town of Yucca Valley, views across to the San Bernardino Mountains, and views back into the monument interior. A bench located at the summit provides a good spot to sit and enjoy the views or a spectacular desert sunset. A trail register is located on the summit. (See Map # 1, Appendix D.)

## 3. BLACK ROCK CANYON

**Type**: x-country, day/overnight
**Mileage**: 5 miles
**Time:** 2 - 3 hours
**Difficulty**: easy
**Elevation Extremes**: 3980' - 4680' **Difference:** 700'
**Starting and Ending Point**: Black Rock Trailhead (3980')
**Topo Maps**: Yucca Valley South 7.5'

Summary: Black Rock Canyon is a pretty, sandy-floored canyon rimmed with plentiful vegetation. The route to the canyon travels gradually uphill through a sandy wash. As the wash narrows and enters the canyon, vegetation changes from a Joshua tree forest to a juniper, oak, and pinyon pine forest. The wash forks at two points in the canyon. Most of the forks gradually lead out of the canyon to higher open areas.

Route: Follow the trail a short distance from the trailboard to Black Rock Canyon Wash. (The R&H trail will branch off this wash). Follow the wash south. The wash branches in several places; stay in the obvious, larger wash. The canyon section of the route is located 1.5 miles from the trailhead. (See Map # 1, Appendix D.)

## 4. WARREN PEAK (5103')

**Type**: x-country, day/overnight
**Mileage**: 6 miles
**Time**: 3 - 4 hours
**Difficulty**: moderately strenuous
**Elevation Extremes**: 3980' - 5103' **Difference:** 1123'
**Starting and Ending Point**: Black Rock Trailhead (3980')
**Topo Maps**: Yucca Valley South 7.5' (1972)

Summary: Excellent views are obtained from the summit of this relatively accessible peak. The approach route through Black Rock Canyon is easy; only the last half-mile of the hike is strenuous. The sweeping views from the summit include the Coachella, Morongo, and Yucca valleys, Mt. San Gorgonio, and Mt. San Jacinto. A climbing register is located on the summit.

Route: Follow the Black Rock Canyon Route (see preceding hike). The wash forks twice in the canyon (1.75 and 2.25 miles from the trailhead). Stay to the right at each of the forks. In the upper part of the canyon, conical Warren Peak will come into view. Follow the wash until it fades out. Climb to the summit via the eastern ridge (to the north). The ground is loose and rocky near the top but not technically difficult. (See Map # 1, Appendix D.)

## 5. LONG CANYON / CHUCKAWALLA BILL RUINS

**Type**: x-country, day/ overnight (note day use area on map)
**Mileage**: 10 miles
**Time**: 6 hours
**Difficulty**: moderate
**Elevation Extremes**: 2510' - 4340' **Difference**: 1830'
**Starting and Ending Point**: Radio Tower Road (4340')
**Topo Maps**: Yucca Valley South 7.5'

Summary: Long Canyon winds down through high mountains. Except for the first half mile, the route gradually loses elevation and walking is easy. The first half mile is rocky and a bit steep but still not difficult. Long Canyon continues all the way to Desert Hot Springs on the south boundary of the monument. An easier alternative to this trip would be to hike one way from the north to the south boundary. This would shorten the trip by one mile and eliminate the uphill return trip. Unfortunately, it would also require a long vehicle shuttle.

About half way down Long Canyon, there is a side wash which leads west to a spring and some ruins. The roofless stone cabin was once occupied by a prospector named Bill Wilson. Wilson was a colorful character who gained many nicknames from his mining partners. He will probably best be remembered by his nickname Chuckawalla Bill. Over the fireplace in the cabin, Wilson wrote this name in the cement "Chuckawalla Bill 1934."

Bill tapped water from a spring not far from the cabin. Today the spring is unreliable as a source of water. However, during wet seasons, water can be found trickling down the slick rocks. Green grasses and bushes thrive in the small, narrow gorge that houses the spring.

Route: Many side washes join Long Canyon Wash. These side washes do not pose a problem while traveling south; however, they may create some confusion on the return trip. It is wise to blaze a route with rock cairns or sand arrows in order to avoid confusion on the return trip.

From the stone drainage ditch on Radio Tower Road, head south down the gully to the bottom of the canyon. Follow the wash down to the south. There is a short cliff section -- about 15 feet of class III (see glossary) -- not far down the wash. It can be avoided by traveling to the right down over a steep slope. Continue in Long Wash to reach Chuckawalla Bill Wash, 4.5 miles from Radio Tower Road. Since there are no outstanding landmarks, locating Chuckawalla Bill Wash can be tricky. Keeping track of progress on a topographical map is the surest way to locate the ruins. In addition, the distant Santa Rosa Mountains can be used as a landmark as follows: Pass through a slick rock chute in the wash. A short distance past the chute, the Santa Rosa Mountains become visible. Farther down the wash they disappear. Eventually, they will reappear at a point where the wash significantly widens. Continue 1/4 mile farther down the wash to reach Chuckawalla Bill Wash.

A slight trace of road can be found along the right (north) of this wide side wash. In addition, there may be some pieces of wood and metal embedded in the sand at the wash junction. (Recent flash flooding may have carried the metal and wood away.) Head west up Chuckawalla Bill Wash to the ruins. The spring is located about 100 yards past the ruins. (See Map # 1, Appendix D.)

To exit the hike on the south boundary, return to the main wash and follow Long Canyon south. Just past the boundary fence is a dirt road. Access to this dirt road by vehicle is from Desert Hot Springs -- drive north off Dillon Road onto Wide Canyon Road. At the end of Wide Canyon Road, follow an unnamed road north to the boundary. (The 7.5' topographical map for this lower portion of the hike is Seven Palms Valley.)

## 6. EUREKA PEAK (5518')

**Type**: x-country/trail, day/overnight
**Mileage**: 5 miles (one-way)
**Time**: 3 - 4 hours
**Difficulty**: moderately strenuous (uphill)
**Elevation Extremes**: 3980' - 5518' **Difference:** 1538'
**Starting Point**: Black Rock Trailhead (3980')
**Ending Point**: Eureka Peak Parking Area (5450')
**Topo Maps**: Yucca Valley South 7.5', Joshua Tree South 7.5'

Summary: Access to this trail is from either Black Rock or Covington Flats. This dual access allows the option of either a one-way or round-trip hike starting from either direction. The route is described from Black Rock to Covington; the excellent views from the peak are the goal and reward of this five-mile hike. Traveling in this north to south direction makes route-finding easier.

The route travels through the hills overlooking Yucca Valley, up a wash, into a narrow canyon, through a pine forest, then up to the summit. (Open areas in the pine forest provide pleasant places for overnight camping.) The view from the summit includes Mt. San Jacinto, Mt. San

Gorgonio, and the Coachella Valley. The view of Mt. San Jacinto towering almost 10,000' above the floor of the Coachella Valley is particularly breathtaking. Both Mt. San Jacinto and Mt. San Gorgonio are frequently capped with snow in the winter and provide a spectacular contrast to the surrounding desert valley.

Route: Orange posts are the official markers for this route. Follow the California Riding and Hiking Trail (brown posts) for approximately two miles. The trail enters a major wash at a point where the wash forks. One fork heads east (R&H); the other heads south. Take the south fork. (There should be an orange post at this junction.) About one-half mile up this wash, there is another fork. Take the smaller wash on the right. Follow the wash to its end in a shallow gully. From here an orange post directs the route up to the left and over a ridge. After reaching the other side of this ridge, head to the right or SSE (another trail heads north). Travel up to a saddle and around to the south side of Eureka Peak. The route joins the trail that leads from Eureka Peak Parking Area up to the peak. At this trail junction, head left 150 yards to the summit or right 100 yards to the parking area. (See Map # 1 & 7, Appendix D.)

## 7. SMITH WATER CANYON

**Type**: x-country/road-trail, day/overnight (note day use area on map)
**Mileage**: 8.5 miles to Quail Springs Picnic Area (one-way)
8.8 miles to West Entrance Wash (one-way)
**Time**: 5 - 7 hours
**Difficulty**: moderate, difficult
**Elevation Extremes**: 4820' - 3660' (QSPA) - 3350' (WEW)
**Difference:** 1160' (QSPA), 1470' (WEW)
**Starting Point**: Covington Flats Backcountry Board (4820')
**Ending Point:** Quail Springs Picnic Area (3979'), West Entrance Wash (3800')
**Topo Maps**: Joshua Tree South 7.5', Indian Cove 7.5'

Summary: Smith Water Canyon is a beautiful, narrow canyon. It is one of the lushest canyons in the monument. The canyon walls rise steeply to high mountain peaks. In the center of the canyon, clear water cascades down through a series of smooth potholes. Several pools lined with bright green algae lie beneath small waterfalls. Tall grasses, cattails, and flowers carpet the sides of the intermittent stream. A grouping of large cottonwoods surrounds the site of a cowboy's camp. At the mouth of the canyon near the junction of Quail Wash, there is a dense, picturesque grove of Joshua trees -- a good camping spot.

Most of the route is fairly straightforward; however, there are some short sections of difficult boulder scrambling in the canyon. A smooth, sloping, 20' high slab spans the wash in the lower end of the canyon. For descending this slab, a 50' length of rope may be desired for use as a retrievable hand line.

Route: From the backcountry board, follow the road-trail east 50 yards and enter a wash. Travel NNE down the wash and through a narrow canyon. Continue following the wash through the open area east of Covington Flats Picnic Area and down into Smith Water Canyon. At the mouth of the canyon (4.5 miles from the Covington Flats Backcountry Board), hike along the east side of the canyon and find an obscure road directly at the base of a hill. Follow this road 1/2 mile to a junction where the route splits. To travel to the West Entrance Wash, head NW (left) to Quail Wash. To travel to Quail Springs Picnic Area, follow the road SE to Quail Springs Road-Trail. (See Chapter 7, Hike # 1.)

For day trips, the route can be shortened 1/2 mile (one-way) by leaving from the Covington Flats Picnic Area. Follow the road-trail east from the picnic area. Turn right at the fork in the road-trail, and continue to the wash. (A marked trail continues across this wash.) At this point, leave the trail and travel NE down the wash into Smith Water Canyon. (See Map # 7, Appendix D.)

## 8. COVINGTON LOOP

**Type**: x-country/trail, day/overnight
**Mileage**: 5.7 mile loop
**Time**: 3-4 hours
**Difficulty**: moderate
**Elevation Extremes**: 4470' - 4890' **Difference**: 420'
**Starting and Ending Points**: Covington Flats Picnic Area (4670')
**Topo Maps**: Joshua Tree South 7.5'

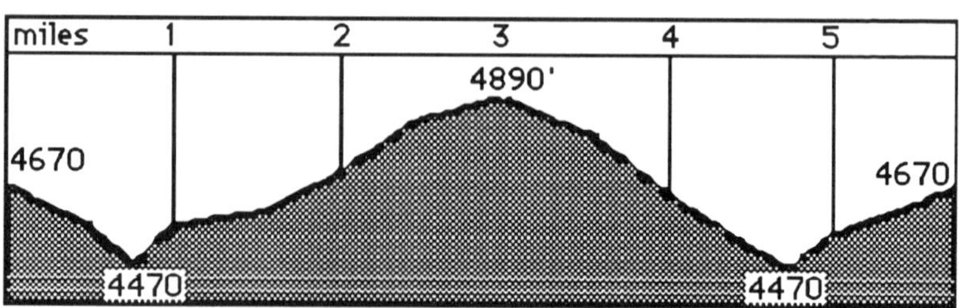


Summary: This hike makes a loop through both Upper and Lower Covington Flats. The route leads through Joshua tree and juniper forested valleys, winds up through pinyon-covered hills, and travels through a narrow canyon. The trail leads past the largest known Joshua tree in the monument (located at Upper Covington Flats, 0.2 miles from the backcountry board). The tree stands about thirty-five feet high and has a circumference of about seventeen feet at the base.

*The largest known Joshua tree in the monument grows at Covington Flats*

A short side trip leads to an interesting mine site. At this site, a 150' section of ore cart track descends from the hillside above the trail. This is the longest know section of track that remains within the monument. At the base of the hill beneath the track are the remains of a drop-bottom ore cart.

Route: Follow the trail southeast from the picnic area to a fork. Take the right fork, the left fork leads to the mine site. The main trail is marked with posts with arrows. The trail intersects the California Riding and Hiking Trail two miles from the picnic area. (Watch for post #28, located near this junction.) At the junction, take a sharp right turn and follow the Riding and Hiking Trail to Upper Covington Flats. Enter the wash located just east of the backcountry board and travel northeast down through the canyon. Intersect the Lower Covington Flats trail and travel northwest up the trail to the picnic area.

The side trip to the mine can be done either at the beginning or at the end of the hike. The turn off to the mine is located about 1/4 mile southwest from the picnic area. Follow the road-trail north from the main trail 0.3 miles. The ore cart and pilings for an elevated track are located at the end of the road-trail. The in-tack section of track is located on the hillside above this location. Climbing the hillside to reach the track is not recommended since the hillside is steep and covered with loose rock and gravel. The track is best viewed from a distance. (See Map # 7, Appendix D.)

## 9. CALIFORNIA RIDING AND HIKING TRAIL

(See Chapter 11)

# Chapter 14

# PARK ROUTE #11

Park Route #11 travels from Pinto Wye to the south boundary of the monument and then on to Interstate 10. This chapter covers the first 22 miles of this 37-mile road. The road travels from the Mojave Desert, through a desert transition zone, then down into the Colorado Desert and the massive expanse of the Pinto Basin.

Hikes originating from Park Route #11 are quite varied in terrain and vegetation. A hike may involve climbing to a high mountain summit, walking along an isolated sandy wash, traveling through a steep-sided canyon, playing on sand dunes, or exploring an area of historic or geologic interest. Backcountry boards are located 2.2 miles (Twin Tanks), 16.2 miles (Turkey Flats), and 21.3 miles (Porcupine Wash) south of Pinto Wye. Belle and White Tank campgrounds are located 1.3 and 2.7 miles south of Pinto Wye. Cottonwood Campground is located nine miles south of the Porcupine Wash Backcountry Board. (See map on page 98.)

## 1. ARCH ROCK NATURE TRAIL / WHITE TANK

(See Chapter 5, Hike # 9.)

## 1. GRAND TANK

**Type**: x-country, day
**Mileage**: 1.25 mile loop
**Time**: 1 hour
**Difficulty**: moderate, easy scrambling
**Elevation Extremes**: fairly level
**Starting and Ending Point**: White Tank Campground, near site # 9
**Topo Maps**: Malapai Hill 7.5'

Summary: Most of the cattle tanks within the monument are filled with sand and maybe an occasional pool of stagnant water. Grand Tank is an exception. It is the largest of the tanks in the eastern half of the monument. It usually holds water throughout the year. During wet seasons it may accumulate as much as 10-15' of water. A short hike leads to this secluded man-made pond.

Route: Follow the Arch Rock Nature Trail (see Chapter 5, Hike # 9) to the "Disappearing Soil" exhibit, one stop past Arch Rock. An eroded, well-beaten path branches off the nature trail and heads ENE. Follow the path across a couple gullies and into a boulder area. The path is easily lost at this point. Continue across a small, bushy hollow and exit left into a larger rock-encircled area. Climb up the boulders along the right side of this area and return to the path beyond the rocks. The path continues a short distance to the tank. To complete the loop, follow the wash below the tank. Continue in the wash until most of the large boulder piles along the right bank have been passed. Climb the right bank and circle around the rock piles to the southern end of the campground.

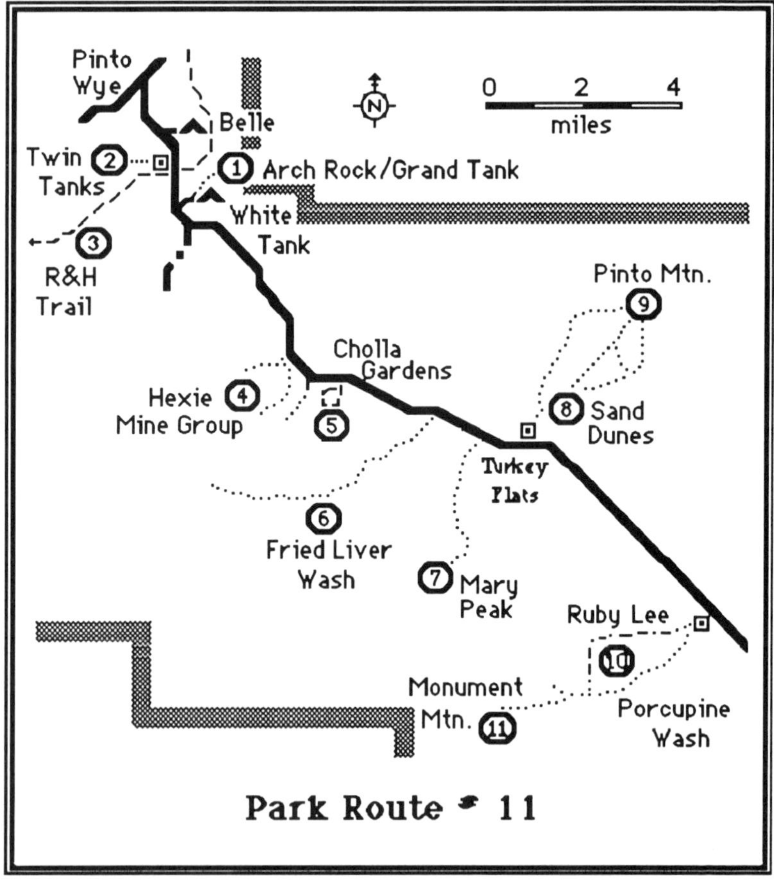


Park Route # 11

*Interpretive signs on the Arch Rock Trail explain the natural creation of this large monzogranite arch. Photo: Kip Knapp*

## 2. TWIN TANKS

**Type**: x-country, day/overnight
**Mileage**: 2 miles round trip to tanks
**Time**: 1 - 2 hours
**Difficulty**: moderate
**Elevation Extremes**: 3900' - 4080' **Difference:** 180'
**Starting and Ending Point**: Twin Tanks Backcountry Board (3900')
**Topo Maps**: Malapai Hill 7.5'

Summary: There are actually five tanks in this area. However, it is the two large man-made tanks which give the area its name. Both of these tanks have a series of natural pothole tanks situated below the rock and cement walls of the man-made tanks.

The Twin Tanks area consists of a maze of narrow, rocky ravines, water-polished slabs, and boulder mounds. Interesting campsite locations can be found within or near this maze.

Route: The tanks can be located by taking a compass bearing of 245° from the backcountry board. Look for a pile of large, bright-white quartz boulders (about one mile distant) along this bearing. Head to the quartz. The quartz boulders sit on a knoll directly above one of the tanks. A man-made dam of rock and mortar can be seen from the quartz pile. To reach the second man-made dam (constructed of cement), travel about 100 yards from the quartz pile on a 300° bearing.

To explore the rocky ravines, continue in the wash past Twin Tanks or travel west from the backcountry board toward the large piles of monzogranite boulders. (See Map # 2, Appendix D.)

## 3. CALIFORNIA RIDING AND HIKING TRAIL

(See Chapter 11)

## 4. HEXIE MINE GROUP

**Type:** x-country/road-trail, day
**Topo Maps:** Fried Liver Wash 7.5'

Summary: A cluster of mining areas lies tucked within the Hexie Mountains not far from the road. The building and mill ruins and open shafts at these areas are reminders of the gold-fever days. (None of the mine shafts in this area have been secured. The shafts are unstable and very dangerous; maintain a safe distance from their openings. Refer to Chapter 3, "Hazards-Use Caution.") This particular section of the Hexies usually has a bountiful floral cactus display in the spring. Descriptions of the individual mines follow:

### 4a. SILVER BELL MINE

**Mileage:** 1 mile
**Time:** 1 hour
**Difficulty:** moderate
**Elevation Extremes:** 2560' - 2880' **Difference:** 320'
**Starting and Ending Point:** pullout just northwest of milepost 8 (2560')

Summary: Silver Bell is the most visible of the mines in this area. From Park Route #11, two wooden ore bins can be seen perched on the side of the hill. The hilltop above the ore bins offers good views of Pinto Basin. Golden Bell Mine lies on the opposite side of the hill. (Travel to Golden Bell is not recommended due to the dangerous open vertical shafts.)

Route: Walk a short distance south from Park Route #11 and find an obscure road-trail. Follow this road-trail to a wash and then up the rocky, eroded hillside beyond the wash. (Note: This mine is pictured and labeled with "Tipples" on the topographical map.)

## 4b. ELDORADO MINE

**Mileage**: 4 miles
**Time**: 2 - 3 hours
**Difficulty**: moderate
**Elevation Extremes**: 2360'- 2640' **Difference:** 280'
**Starting and Ending Point**: pullout just northwest of milepost 8 (2560')

Summary: This is the largest of the Hexie mining areas. Eldorado Mine is historically noteworthy because it supplied a greater variety of minerals than any other mine in the monument. The remains of two concrete vats lie in the wash beneath the mine. One house structure still stands.

Route: Travel southeast from the parking area and circle around the base of the hill. Head west up the second wash and travel approximately 1/2 mile to the mine. Continuing up the wash will lead to Pleasant Valley (see Chapter 9).

## 4c. GOLDEN BEE

**Mileage**: 3.5 miles
**Time**: 2 - 3 hours
**Difficulty**: moderately strenuous
**Elevation Extremes**: 2200' - 2840' **Difference:** 640'
**Starting and Ending Point**: 1/4 mile northwest of Cholla Cactus Garden (2280')

Summary: This mine operated for a short period in the late 1930's. There were once many buildings at the site. Today all that remains standing are parts of the ore bins and a short wooden head frame.

Route: Park on the southeast side of Park Route #11 at a blocked-off road-trail. The road-trail to the mine is fairly easy to follow except for a section through the wash. The trail can again be easily found on the other side of the wash.

## 5. CHOLLA CACTUS GARDEN

(See Chapter 5, Hike # 10.)

## 6. FRIED LIVER WASH - (See Chapter 9, Hike # 7.)

## 7. MARY PEAK (3820')

**Type**: x-country, day/overnight
**Mileage**: 6.5 miles
**Time**: 4 - 6 hours
**Difficulty**: strenuous, moderately difficult
**Elevation Extremes**: 1756' - 3820' **Difference:** 2064'
**Starting & Ending Point**: Park Route #11, 1 mile south of milepost 14
**Topo Maps**: Pinto Mountain 7.5' / Porcupine Wash 7.5' or Hexie Mountains 15'

Summary: Mary Peak, a dome shaped mountain with a 1000'+ rocky cliff face, is the most extreme-looking mountain in the monument. The mountain's rugged appearance suggests that this hike should be reserved for those with technical climbing ability. However, the climb to the summit is relatively straightforward and requires no special technical skills. The summit and ascent ridges provide commanding views of the Pinto Basin and the Pinto and Coxcomb mountains.

Route: Head S from Park Route #11 to the base of the narrow ridge which lies just east and parallel to a major wash. Hike up the nose of the ridge and travel along the ridgetop. The ridge, which sits directly adjacent to the cliff face, provides impressive views of the rocky cliffs.

In a few places on the lower mountain, the ridgetop is narrow and bladelike. It is necessary to negotiate a route through the large rock chunks which make up the top of the ridge. As the ridge curves to the east, it broadens making travel a little easier. Follow the ridge as it curves around the east side of the peak then west to the summit.

Alternate Routes: For a longer, gentler climb, travel up the next ridge to the east of the above described route. This route only adds about 1/2 mile to the trip one way. The drawback is the loss of the rocky cliff views on the ascent.

To make a loop trip and add variety of terrain, descend southwest down the back side of the peak into a wash. Follow the wash down and around the west side of the mountain to the front of the peak. This adds about 1.25 miles to the trip. (Note: The descent route down the wash involves traveling through a canyon over smooth granite. Use caution travelling on this slippery surface.)

## 8. SAND DUNES

**Type**: x-country, day/overnight
**Mileage**: 2 miles
**Time**: 1 hour
**Difficulty**: easy
**Elevation Extremes**: 1720' - 1820' **Difference:** 100'
**Starting and Ending Point**: Turkey Flats Backcountry Board (1791')
**Topo Maps:** Pinto Mountain 7.5'

Summary: At the base of the mountains, along the northern edge of Pinto Basin, there lies a low ridge of wind-swept sand dunes, reminders of the harsh desert environment. Spring is the best time to visit the dunes. It is a time when dune primrose carpet the area. Spring at the dunes is also the best time and place to view the graceful desert lily. Moved by spring breezes, the slender leaves of the lilies draw circles in the sand around the large white flowers.

Route: From the backcountry board, head NNE to the obvious sandy ridge. (See topographical map on page 105.)

## 9. PINTO MOUNTAIN (3983')

**Type:** x-country, day/overnight
**Mileage**: South Wash -- 9 miles
West Wash -- 12 miles
Southeast Wash -- 13 miles
**Time:** 7 - 10 hours
**Difficulty**: strenuous, difficult
**Elevation Extremes**: 1600' - 3983' **Difference:** 2383'
**Starting and Ending Point**: Turkey Flats Backcountry Board (1791')
**Topo Maps**: Pinto Mountain 7.5'

Summary: Pinto Mountain towers 2300' above the broad, flat Pinto Basin. The climb to the summit is rugged, strenuous, and much more difficult than it appears from the road. Views from the summit and approach ridges provide excellent panoramas of the Pinto Basin and surrounding mountains. The best logic for climbing this mountain is to use the washes for approaches and to gain the ridges as soon as possible to attain better views. The climb is commonly done as an overnight trip. Camp is usually set up at the base of the mountain. There is a climbing register located within the 7' high cairn that marks the summit.

South Wash: This is the most rugged of the three routes, but it is also the shortest and most direct. Walk NNE to the east edge of the dunes and travel through a gap between the dunes and a low dark ridge. From here head N to the obvious canyon/wash. Pinto summit can be seen above this wash. Follow the wash as it winds up through a steep canyon. Low, smooth-surfaced rock walls span the width of the wash requiring short sections of climbing (class III). Stay in the wash for about one mile. Watch the right ridge for an obvious change in rock color. Climb out of the wash to the right at a point where the ridge is whitened by a quartz outcrop. Travel along the ridgetop. Move to the right (west) of the ridge to climb up through the last rocky mound before the summit plateau. The plateau gradually rises to the summit. (See topographical map on page 105.)

West Wash: Of the three routes described, the west wash provides the most straightforward route to the summit. Staying in the wash, rather than climbing the ridges, makes this a less-difficult trip. Head NNW from the backcountry board to the western base of the mountain. Travel between the base of the mountain and two small hills to the west. Head east up the wide wash. The wash eventually narrows and splits; take the right fork -- the wider and less rocky of the two forks. In the upper steep section of the wash, there is another split. Keep right and follow the wash/gully the remaining way to the summit plateau. (See topographical map on page 105.)

Southeast Wash: This route is the easiest but longest of the three routes. From the gap at the dunes (see South Wash), head ENE approximately two miles to a large, open wash. (The wash is not visible from

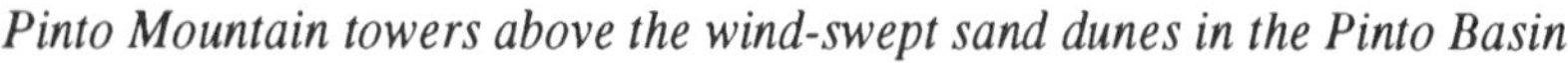

*Pinto Mountain towers above the wind-swept sand dunes in the Pinto Basin*

*USGS topographical map: Hexie Mountains 15' (1663)*

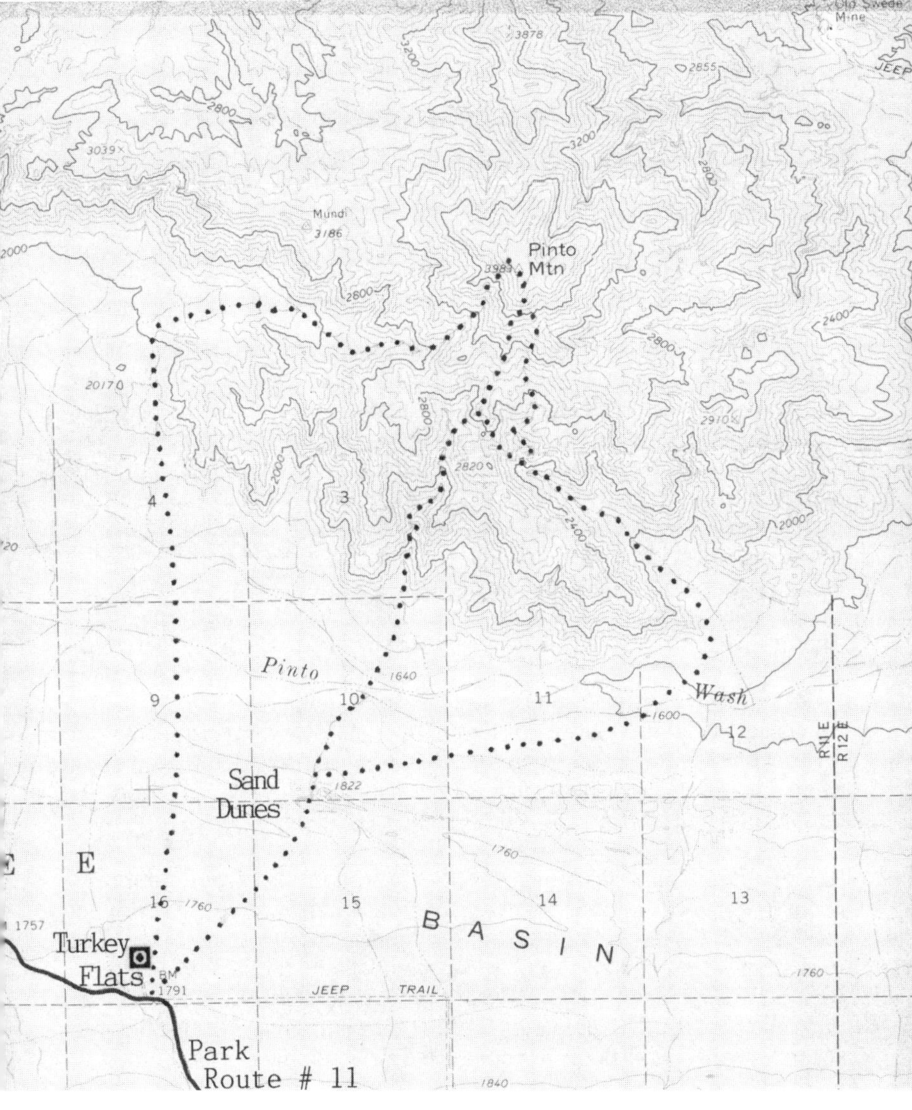


the gap.) Travel up along the left (southwest) side of the wash and into a canyon. The incline is fairly gradual with few boulder obstructions. Approximately 1.5 miles up the wash, the canyon narrows and bends to the northeast. Climb northwest up a steep draw to a ridgetop (this is the same ridgetop described in the South Wash route), or continue following the wash for a lower, longer hike. For the latter choice, follow the wash as far as possible, then continue hiking up the final steep section to the summit. (See topographical map page 105.)

## 10. PORCUPINE WASH / RUBY LEE MILL SITE

**Type**: road-trail/x-country, day/overnight
**Mileage**: 8.5 mile loop
**Time**: 5 - 6 hours
**Difficulty**: moderate
**Elevation Extremes**: 2400' - 3160' **Difference:** 760'
**Starting & Ending Point**: Porcupine Wash Backcountry Board (2400')
**Topo Maps**: Porcupine Wash 7.5'

Summary: This is a pleasant loop hike which provides a variety of terrain and some historical and natural highlights. The route travels up an alluvial fan, from where there are good views of the Pinto Basin, and returns via a narrow canyon, a good location for viewing birds and early-spring wildflowers. Historical points of interest include Indian petroglyphs and the Ruby Lee Mill Site.

At one time, there was a small house at the Ruby Lee site. Today, the only testimony to the mill's existence is a pile of ore, a roofless rock shelter filled with debris, and an inscription, "Ruby Lee Mill Site 1935." The inscription is carved on a large round boulder which sits above the site.

A side trip from the loop continues up Porcupine Wash, through a canyon, to a broad valley. An intermittent jeep trail travels up the valley into the mountains where mine shafts are located. Monument Mountain rises above the center of the valley. The side trip from the loop to the mines is an additional 5.5 miles one-way.

Route: From the backcountry board, follow the road-trail southwest about 1/4 mile to an old borrow pit. From the pit, head WSW toward the base of the hills (follow a line of green and white stakes). This route will intersect a road-trail which parallels the mountains and heads west to Ruby Lee. The road-trail is difficult to follow in sections through the wash. If necessary, follow the wash until it separates into several smaller washes (at the end of the first grouping of hills) then locate the road-trail again. About 3 miles from the parking area, the road-trail makes a sharp bend to the right (north). From here, continue a short distance to reach the rocky cove where the mill site is located.

To continue the loop, follow the road-trail west past Ruby Lee. The route beyond the mill site is not as well defined as the route leading up to the mill site. The center of the road-trail is largely overgrown. It will take time and a discerning eye to stay on the trail.

If it becomes too difficult to follow the road-trail, travel down any of the washes in the area. All the washes lead down into Porcupine Wash.

The road-trail, however, provides the easiest and gentlest route through the rugged boulder field which lies between Ruby Lee and Porcupine Wash.

The road-trail eventually takes a bend to the south, follows the base of the hills, then descends into Porcupine Wash. (Traveling west up the wash will lead to the broad valley below Monument Mountain.) To complete the loop, follow Porcupine Wash east through a canyon and back to Park Route #11. The wash exits onto the road about 100 feet southwest of the backcountry board. The petroglyphs are located approximately 200 yards southwest of the roadway on a large rock which sits on the north edge of Porcupine Wash. (See Map # 8, Appendix D.)

## 11. MONUMENT MOUNTAIN (4834')

**Type**: x-country, day/overnight
**Mileage**: 20 miles
**Time:** 12 - 14 hours
**Difficulty**: strenuous, moderately difficult
**Elevation Extremes**: 2400' - 4834' **Difference:** 2434'
**Starting & Ending Point**: Porcupine Wash Backcountry Board (2400')
**Topo Maps**: Porcupine Wash 7.5', Washington Wash 7.5'

Summary: Monument Mountain is rightly named both because of its shape and because of the view obtained from the summit. The mountain, which is the highest peak in the Hexie Mountains, appears as a pointed cone resting upon a broad pedestal. It is one of the most distinctive-looking peaks in the monument. A long approach, followed by a steep rocky climb, leads to excellent views of a major portion of the monument. There is a climbing register on the summit. (For an alternative route see Chapter 15, Hike # 1.)

Route: Travel SSW 200 yards to the end of a short road-trail. Head WSW 100 yards to the deepest section of Porcupine Wash. Travel up the wash, through a canyon, to a broad upper valley where Monument Mountain can be seen to the southwest. Continue following the main wash until the summit cone of Monument Mountain appears to lower beneath the closer ridges. Leave the wash and travel to the base of the mountain.

There are four distinct drainages on this side of Monument Mountain. The two center drainages form a narrow 'V'. Climb the ridge between the 'V' for the most gradual, short ascent to the top of a rise. From the top of this rise, drop down into a wash (approximately 80'). Walk up the wash a short distance. Climb toward the summit along the right side of the gully that descends from the mountain top. At the upper elevations, angle further to the right (SW) for easier climbing. (See Map # 8, Appendix D.)

# Chapter 15

# COTTONWOOD

Cottonwood lies in the southernmost section of the monument. The vegetation and terrain of the area, which is within the Colorado Desert, are quite different from that of the higher Mojave Desert. Joshua trees are replaced by smoke trees, palo verdes, and palm trees. Generally, more flowers can be found here in the low desert rather than in the higher Mojave Desert. Cottonwood is known for having some of the best spring wildflower displays in the monument.

The area is most easily accessed from Interstate 10, about one mile south of the South Entrance. The area can also be reached by traveling south on Park Route #11 from Pinto Wye. Hikes originating from this area lead to rugged high peaks, as well as to less rugged, lower peaks; to areas of historical interest; along gentle trails and washes; and to the largest palm oases in the monument. A backcountry board is located at the end of Cottonwood Springs Road. Cottonwood Campground, which has 62 sites, is the only campground in the area. A visitor center is located on Park Route #11 just north of the Cottonwood Springs Road.

## 1. MONUMENT MOUNTAIN (4834')

**Type:** x-country, day/overnight
**Mileage:** 6 miles
**Time:** 5 - 6 hours
**Difficulty:** strenuous, moderately difficult
**Elevation Extremes:** 3240' - 4834' **Difference:** 1594'
**Starting and Ending Point:** Pinkham Road (5 miles from Park Route #11)
**Topo Maps:** Washington Wash 7.5'

Summary: Monument Mountain is the highest peak in the Hexie Mountains. Excellent views of the monument are the reward for completing the rugged hike to the summit. There are a few places suitable for camping on the rocky ridges; however, camping is better at the base of the mountain where the ground is level and sandy. A four-wheel drive vehicle is required to reach the starting point of this hike.

Route: The shortest, most gradual route to the summit of Monument Mountain is up the mountain's southeast ridge. This is the ridge seen on the horizon from the starting point on Pinkham Road. Attain the ridge by heading north up one of the three lower, south-facing ridges. Climb (northwest) up the main southeast ridge to a high point. This high point deceivingly appears to be the summit. The true summit of Monument Mountain, which appears as a pointed cone, can be seen from the top of this high point. Follow the ridge as it bends to the north and continue to the base of the summit cone. A steep, unavoidable scramble leads up the rocky cone to the true summit. A climbing register is located on the peak. (See Chapter 14, Hike # 11, for an alternative route. See Map # 8, Appendix D.)

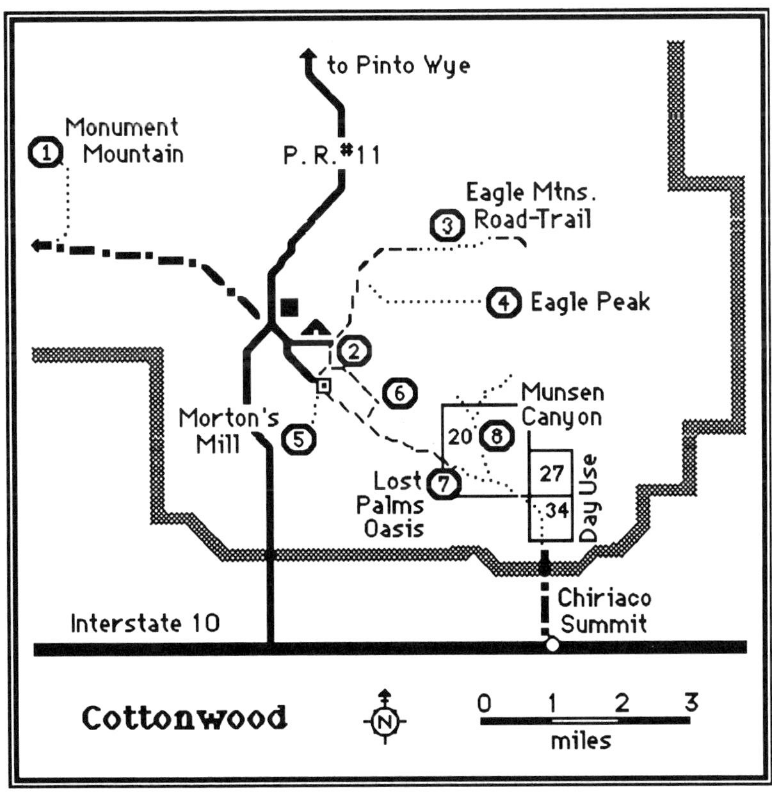


## 2. COTTONWOOD NATURE TRAIL

(See Chapter 5, Hike # 11.)

## 3. EAGLE MOUNTAINS ROAD-TRAIL

**Type**: road-trail/x-country, day/overnight
**Mileage**: 11 miles round trip to Conejo Well cutoff
**Time**: 5 - 6 hours
**Difficulty**: easy
**Elevation Extremes**: 3000' - 3400' **Difference:** 400'
**Starting and Ending Point**: Cottonwood Springs Oasis (3000')
**Topo Maps**: Porcupine Wash 7.5', Conejo Well 7.5', Cottonwood Spring 7.5'

Summary: This hike is a good choice for an easy overnight trip to a remote area within the Colorado Desert. The road-trail travels around the base of Eagle Peak, through the western end of the Eagle Mountains, and into the south portion of Pinto Basin. The yuccas are particularly dense on the northwest side of Eagle Peak; they provide a beautiful floral display in the spring. The trail is easy to follow except in a few sections that cross or follow a wash.

Route: Hike the Cottonwood Nature Trail (see Chapter 5, Hike # 11) from Cottonwood Oasis to the campground. The road-trail begins at site 17, Loop B. Travel the road-trail to a gap in the Eagle Mountains. At this point, the road-trail enters and becomes lost in a wash. Follow the wash through the mountains. The road-trail can again be found on the west side of the mountains. The road-trail continues along the base of Eagle Peak, passes the road to Conejo Well, and then veers north. (Note: This road-trail is pictured on 15' maps - Cottonwood Spring, Hexie Mountains, Pinto Basin - but not 7.5' maps.)

## 4. EAGLE PEAK (5350')

**Type:** road-trail/x-country, day/overnight
**Mileage:** 10 miles
**Time:** 8 - 10 hours
**Difficulty:** strenuous, difficult
**Elevation Extremes:** 3000' - 5350' **Difference:** 2350'
**Starting and Ending Point:** Cottonwood Springs Oasis (3000')
**Topo Maps:** Porcupine Wash 7.5', Cottonwood Spring 7.5', Hayfield 7.5', Conejo Well 7.5'

Summary: Eagle Peak is one of the most rugged mountains in the monument. The climb to the summit is steep and rocky. However, the view from the summit is among one of the best views in the monument. Pinto Basin, Mt. San Gorgonio, Mt. San Jacinto, Pinkham Canyon, and the Hexie, Pinto, Cottonwood, and Eagle Mountain ranges are a few of the highlights included in the unobstructed, 360° view.

On the climb to the summit, note the dramatic change in vegetation throughout the 2,350 feet of elevation gain. Vegetation around the base of the peak is predominantly creosote, yucca, and cholla. At the cool upper elevations of the mountain, oak, juniper, and pinyon pine abound. A climbing register is located on the summit.

Route: Follow the Eagle Mountains Road-Trail (see preceding hike) 1.5 to 2 miles; then head E toward Eagle Peak. Navigate through the boulders and gullies to the base of the deep ravine on the mountain. (Heading toward the ravine before traveling the suggested 1.5 miles on the road-trail will make the hike more difficult. A greater amount of gullies and boulders are located at the more southern base of the mountain.) Scramble up through bushes and boulders to the center of the ravine where a rocky wash provides easier traveling. Follow the ravine to a false summit. From here the true summit can be seen to the ESE. Bushwhack and scramble over rocky, densely-vegetated terrain to reach the gentle, west-facing slope that leads to the summit.

Note: From the summit, it looks like there is an easier and more straightforward route on the north side of Eagle Peak through Conejo Well. This is an illusion to say the least. The northern route does provide an easier approach to the base. In addition, the scramble from the false summit to the real summit is avoided. However, the actual climb up the mountain is more difficult, route finding is more difficult, and the route is three miles longer one-way.

*Camping at the base of the Eagle Mountains*

## 5. MORTON'S MILL / LITTLE CHILCOOT PASS

**Type:** x-country, day
**Mileage:** 1 mile
**Time:** 1 hour
**Difficulty:** easy
**Elevation Extremes:** 2800' - 3000' **Difference:** 200'
**Starting and Ending Point:** Cottonwood Springs Oasis (3000')
**Topo Map:** Cottonwood Spring 7.5'

Summary: A hike over the old teamster's route and through a wash leads to the site of a stamp mill that operated in the 1930's. The remains at Morton's Mill, which include a foundation, an old vehicle, and some rusted tanks, are meager. However, it is the route to the mill site, and not the mill site itself, that makes this hike interesting. The route travels through a wash which is rich with Colorado Desert flora. Mesquite, palo verdes, smoke trees, and yuccas dominate the vegetation.

The teamster's route was the wagon road used to reach Cottonwood Springs in the early 1900's. The majority of the teamster's route has vanished. However, a short section of the road known as "Little Chilcoot Pass" can still be seen along the wash that leads to the mill site. Little Chilcoot Pass was built to bypass a low cliff in the wash.

Route: Follow the wash south from Cottonwood Springs. The route is marked with wooden posts. Travel over Little Chilcoot Pass, 1/4 mile from Cottonwood Springs, and continue down the wash to Morton's Mill. The mill site is located along the right side of the wash at the base of a hill. An arrow on a wooden post in the wash points to the site. (Note: The mill site is not marked on USGS topographical maps. See Map # 9, Appendix D.)

## 6. MASTODON PEAK LOOP

**Type**: trail, day
**Mileage**: 3 mile loop
**Time**: 2 hours
**Difficulty**: moderate, moderate scrambling up the peak
**Elevation Extremes**: 3000' - 3440' **Difference:** 440'
**Starting and Ending Point**: Cottonwood Springs Oasis (3000')
**Topo Maps**: Cottonwood Spring 7.5'

Summary: The Mastodon loop travels past two sites that were busy during the mining days. Traveling counter clockwise from Cottonwood Springs, the trail passes Mastodon Mine and then the Winona Mill site. The Mastodon Mine was a gold mine which operated between 1919 and 1932. The open mine shafts can still be seen today. (Do not enter mine shafts. They are unstable and dangerous. Refer to Chapter 3, "Hazards-Use Caution.")

Mastodon Peak lies just above the mine. Invite your imagination to mimic that of the early prospectors who named this peak. They imagined the rock formation which creates the peak to be a likeness of a prehistoric elephant head. A short spur-trail leads to the summit of the peak; the trail begins just southeast of the mine. The impressive views from Mastodon Peak include the Cottonwood area, Eagle Peak, Monument Mountain, Mt. San Jacinto, Shavers Valley, and the Salton Sea.

Less than a mile past Mastodon Mine lies Winona Mill. Winona was the site of a small village and mill that was active in the 1920's. The foundations of the mill buildings still dot the hillside. A thick grouping of cottonwoods and exotic trees and shrubs, which were planted by the millhands, flourishes in a wash at the base of the hill. The large trees provide habitat for birds and wildlife and shade for passing hikers. The loop continues from Winona back to the Cottonwood Springs Parking Lot. (See Map # 9, Appendix D.)

## 7. LOST PALMS OASIS

**Type**: trail, day/overnight (note day use area on map)
**Mileage**: 7.5 miles
**Time**: 4 - 6 hours
**Difficulty:** moderate (to the oasis overlook)
**Elevation Extremes**: 3000' - 3440' **Difference:** 440'
**Starting and Ending Point**: Cottonwood Springs Oasis (3000')
**Topo Maps**: Cottonwood Spring 7.5'

Summary: Lost Palms Oasis is one of the two largest palm oases in the monument. It rivals Munsen Canyon in the number of palms in one canyon (more than 100 palms in each canyon). However, Lost Palms Oasis has a larger concentration of palms in a single area.

The trail to the oasis overlook travels through sandy washes and rolling hills. The overlook is the end of the "moderate" portion of the hike. A steep, rugged, strenuous trail leads down to the oasis and canyon bottom. Beneath the towering fan palms, water trickles down through the sandy wash to a rocky boulder canyon farther down the wash. The echoing of the canyon wren's song and the rustling of the palms add to the beauty of this remote area. In the upper end of the oasis, there is a rugged, boulder-strewn side canyon which leads to Dike Springs and more palm stands.

Watch for animal tracks and droppings along the trail and in the canyon bottom. The combination of the water, rugged terrain, and remoteness of the area makes Lost Palms Oasis ideal habitat for the elusive bighorn sheep. Although overnight camping is not permitted at the oasis, camping is allowed in the rolling hills before the overlook. (See

Map # 9, Appendix D. Note the day use area. Refer to Chapter 3, "Understanding Day Use Areas And Desert Bighorn Sheep.")

*Lost Palms Oasis*

Victory Palms (2680'): Hiking one mile down the wash from Lost Palms Oasis leads to Victory Palms (only two palms). These palms can be reached either by traveling down through the canyon -- which involves some difficult, though interesting, boulder scrambling -- or by following an obscure trail along the south side of the canyon. To find the trail, follow the wash downhill 0.2 miles from Lost Palms Oasis. Look for a cairn; it marks the point where the trail leaves the right (southwest) side of the wash. A Cottonwood Spring 15' topographical map is helpful for finding and following this trail. (The trail is marked in a slightly different location on the 7.5' map.)

## 8. MUNSEN CANYON

**Type**: x-country, day/overnight (note day use area on map)
**Mileage**: 9 miles round trip to main oasis
(12 miles round trip to uppermost oasis)
**Time**: 7 - 10 hours, (9 - 12 hours)
**Difficulty**: strenuous, difficult
**Elevation Extremes**: 1880' - 3280' (4200') **Difference:** 1400' (2320')
**Starting and Ending Point**: south boundary above Chiriaco Summit (1880')
**Topo Maps**: Hayfield 7.5', Cottonwood Spring 7.5'

Summary: This canyon has all the beauty and life of Lost Palms Canyon but on a larger scale. With over 110 palms, this canyon surpasses Lost Palms in the number of palms in one canyon. The palm stands, which contain up to thirty-five trees, are spread out over a two-mile stretch within the canyon. Small stands of palms are interspersed between and beyond the two large palm groves which are located at Summit Springs and Munsen Oasis.

One of the most picturesque palm groves is located in an upper side canyon. Large rock formations surround this remote grouping of fifteen palms. Travel up this side canyon involves some of the most difficult boulder scrambling (difficult+) of the entire hike.

The remote location and rugged terrain of Munsen Canyon create a haven for wildlife. The seclusive bighorn sheep inhabit the upper reaches of the canyon. Because it is bighorn habitat, the canyon is included within a day use area. (Refer to Chapter 3, "Understanding Day Use Areas And Desert Bighorn Sheep.") Camping is allowed either near the beginning of the hike or in the upper side canyon past the last palm stand. Reaching the latter location with a full backpack is very difficult and not recommended.

Route: A dirt road leads north from Chiriaco Summit into the monument. The road is closed to vehicles about 1/4 mile north of the monument boundary. Park at the road closure and hike up the road which soon disappears in a large sandy wash. Continue following the wash into a canyon. The canyon forks three miles from the boundary. Take the right fork. The left fork leads to Victory Palms (refer to the preceding hike, Lost Palms Oasis).

At this point, travel changes from easy to difficult. The canyon is filled with large boulders. Confidence in boulder scrambling is a must for continuing on this route. Summit Springs, the first of the two large palm groves, lies about 1/2 mile above this fork. Travel is easier between Summit Springs and Munsen Oasis, the largest palm grove in the canyon. However, there are still several boulder obstructions in this one mile section.

About 0.4 miles beyond Munsen Oasis, there is a side canyon. (A stand of fourteen palms grows at this junction.) This eastern side canyon leads to the picturesque grouping of fifteen palms noted in the hike summary. The side canyon eventually opens up to a rocky valley below Eagle Peak. (See Map # 9, Appendix D.)

*Munsen Canyon leads to a rocky valley below Eagle Peak*

# Chapter 16

# WONDERLAND OF ROCKS

The Wonderland of Rocks is one of the most incredible areas within the monument. Twelve square miles of massive monzogranite boulder piles create this jumbled maze. Within this stony wilderness, there are miniature Joshua tree forests tucked in verdant valleys; large willows surrounding ponds that attract a myriad of birds and other wildlife; sandy washes lined with giant flowering nolinas; intermittent streams flowing through a series of caves created by the haphazard lay of the boulders; and several small, clear pools of water that reflect the beautiful surroundings.

Travel through the Wonderland is difficult, except in a few sandy washes that cut into the outer edge of the area. Solo travel is highly discouraged except in the easier, established routes in the washes. A hiker who slips off a boulder while traveling down one of the many gullies could fall through a series of cracks and dropoffs created by the several layers of boulders. The maze-like nature of the Wonderland has proven to be both a prison for those lost or injured in the area and a difficult puzzle for those searching for the lost or injured. Proficient map and compass skills are essential for anyone venturing into the Wonderland.

The Wonderland can be accessed from either Park Route #12 or Indian Cove. Nearby campgrounds include Indian Cove, Hidden Valley, and Ryan. Backcountry boards are located at Indian Cove and at Keys West Gate. Due to a resident population of bighorn sheep, most of the Wonderland is included in a day use area. Camping is allowed along the outer edges of the Wonderland outside the restricted area. (Camping in the day use area is harmful to the bighorn. Refer to Chapter 3, "Understanding Day Use Areas And Desert Bighorn Sheep.") See map on page 119.

## 1. THE BIG BARKER DAM LOOP

(See Chapter 8, Hike # 1.)

*Barker Dam creates a small, beautiful lake within the Wonderland*

## 2. WONDERLAND RANCH WASH

**Type**: x-country, day
**Mileage**: 2 miles round trip to Astro Domes
**Time**: 1.5 hours
**Difficulty**: easy, easy scrambling
**Elevation Extremes**: relatively level
**Starting and Ending Point**: Wonderland Ranch Parking Area (4280')
**Topo Map:** Indian Cove 7.5'

Summary: This popular route is frequently used by rock climbers traveling to the Astro Domes. The Astro Domes are a collection of giant, steep-faced boulders that provide climbers with some of the highest, most extreme climbs in the monument. Some of these boulders tower over 300' above the wash. This hike provides an opportunity both to view some of these climbing extremists and to enjoy the natural beauty of the area. Several washes and canyons branch from this valley and lead to equally interesting, but confusing, maze-like areas.

Route: Follow the road-trail from the parking area to the ruins of a pink house (the former Wonderland Ranch). Head SW from the front corner of the house and enter a wash fifty feet away. Travel northwest up the wash. (Look for the cold storage compartment, built under an overhanging boulder, and an Indian bedrock mortar located about 25 yards up the wash on the left side.) Follow the wash and the intermittent parallel trail as they wind around the bushes and boulders in the rocky corridor. The wash emerges in the valley below the Astro Domes. (See Map # 3, Appendix D.)

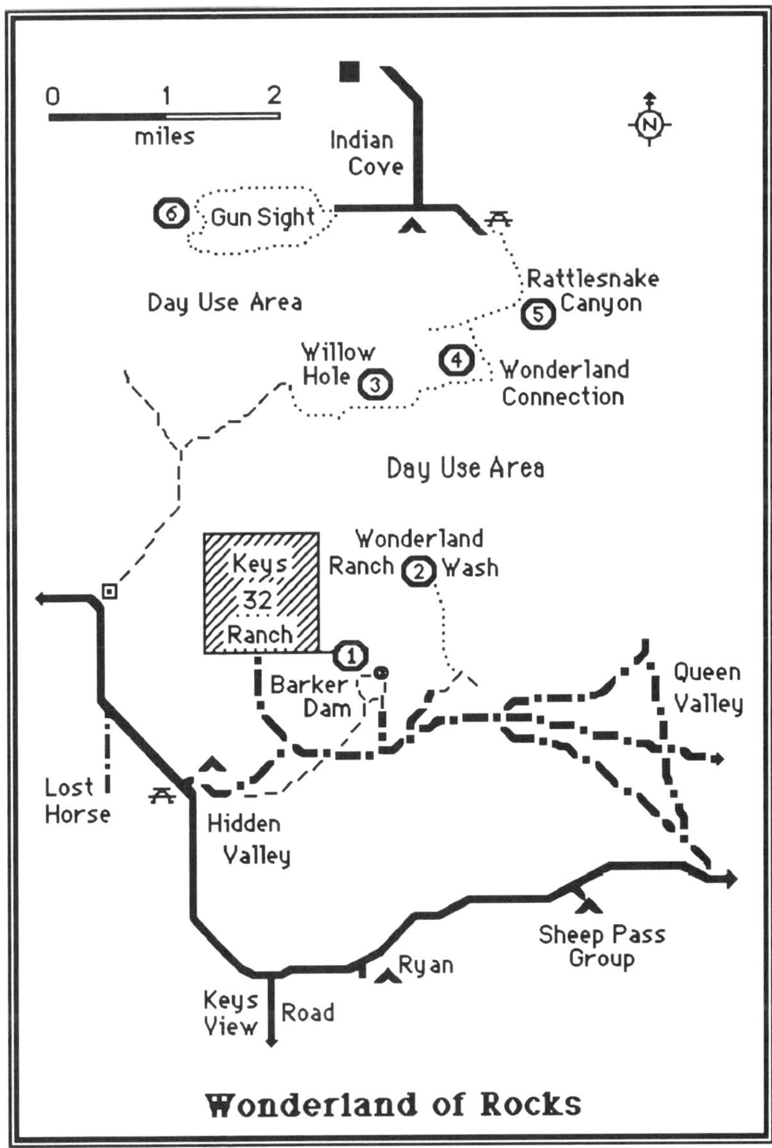

## 3. WILLOW HOLE

**Type:** trail/x-country, day
**Mileage:** 7 miles
**Time:** 4 hours
**Difficulty:** easy
**Elevation Extremes:** 4020' - 4140' **Difference:** 120'
**Starting and Ending Point:** Keys West Gate (4040')
**Topo Map:** Indian Cove 7.5'

Summary: This is one of the easiest and most popular hiking routes into the Wonderland. The route travels through open desert then follows a wash which narrows as it winds through tall boulder piles. The wash widens just before Willow Hole where big willow trees and rocky walls surround large pools of water.

Route: Follow the trail north 1.4 miles from the parking area to a fork in the trail. The left trail, marked with the sign, "Horse and Foot Trail," is the Boy Scout Trail. Take the right trail. Follow the trail until it disappears in the wash. Continue down the wash through a rocky corridor to Willow Hole. (See Map # 3 & 6, Appendix D.)

*A hiker in Wonderland Ranch Wash looks for climbers on the South Astro Dome*

## 4. WONDERLAND CONNECTION

**Type**: trail/x-country, day
**Mileage**: 5.5 miles one-way
**Time**: 6 hours
**Difficulty**: strenuous, difficult (+)
**Elevation Extremes**: 3017' - 4140' **Difference:** 1123'
**Starting Point**: Keys West Gate (4040')
**Ending Point**: Indian Cove Picnic Area (3017')
**Topo Map**: Indian Cove 7.5'

Summary: This route passes through the heart of the Wonderland as it leads from Willow Hole to Indian Cove. The route follows a rocky wash where flowing water and small pools can be found throughout much of the year. It passes near boulder caves and through small valleys, including the valley where Oh-bay-yo-yo is located.

Since the early 1940's, local people have been using the Oh-bay-yo-yo cave as a wilderness retreat. The cave is actually no more than a hollow under a boulder with walls constructed of sticks and rocks. However, these early hikers took pride (and still do) in their secluded fort. They kept a register in the cave. It was traditional for hikers to enter their name in the log along with the number of times they had completed the trek to Oh-bay-yo-yo.

The locals went to great pains to build the cave and to keep it well stocked with supplies. One of the original builders of the cave made a log entry announcing that he had carried fifty pounds of flat rocks uphill from Indian Cove to build one of the cave walls. The fort was stocked with dishes, pans, food, matches, a lamp, and a Bible. The original register, as well as many of the supplies that were kept in the fort, has since disappeared. (Please leave what little remains at the retreat.)

This hike through the Wonderland is beautiful and rewarding; however, the rugged terrain makes travel difficult and time-consuming. The route travels through a slick rock canyon with pools of water and giant rock slabs to crawl around, over, or under. Don't be deceived by the fact that this hike is all downhill - allow plenty of time to complete the trip. (Camping is not allowed in the Wonderland. Refer to Chapter 3, "Understanding Day Use Areas And Desert Bighorn Sheep.")

Route: Hike to Willow Hole (see preceding hike) and exit the wash on the right side. Travel through the south half of the willow grove to reach a small cove at the rear of the grove. Travel 50' along a well beaten path on the right side of the cove to reach the top of a low ridge. (See map drawing on page 122.) From the top of the ridge, head E 100 yards through a relatively flat, open area to reach a gap between two rock piles. Climb down through the gap and drop into a narrow boulder-strewn wash. Follow the course of the wash through the rocks. Continue following the wash as it makes a sharp bend to the left* and then to the right. The wash becomes boulder-clogged; further travel involves difficult rock scrambling. (* Use caution at this turn. There is a tendency to miss the turn, exit the wash, and travel *up* into an open area. After leaving the low ridge above Willow Hole, all travel should be *downhill.*)

About 0.7 miles from Willow Hole, the wash intersects a north/south wash. Just before this intersection, there is an open, flat area. From here a trail leads to the left (north) to Oh-bay-yo-yo. Traveling north in the north/south wash will lead to the upper sections of Rattlesnake Canyon. (The last section of the north/south wash is steep and travel is very difficult.) Head NE down Rattlesnake Canyon. See Chapter 12, Hike # 5, for the description of the remaining hike to Indian Cove. (See Map # 6, Appendix D.)

*Wonderland Connection: route through Willow Hole*

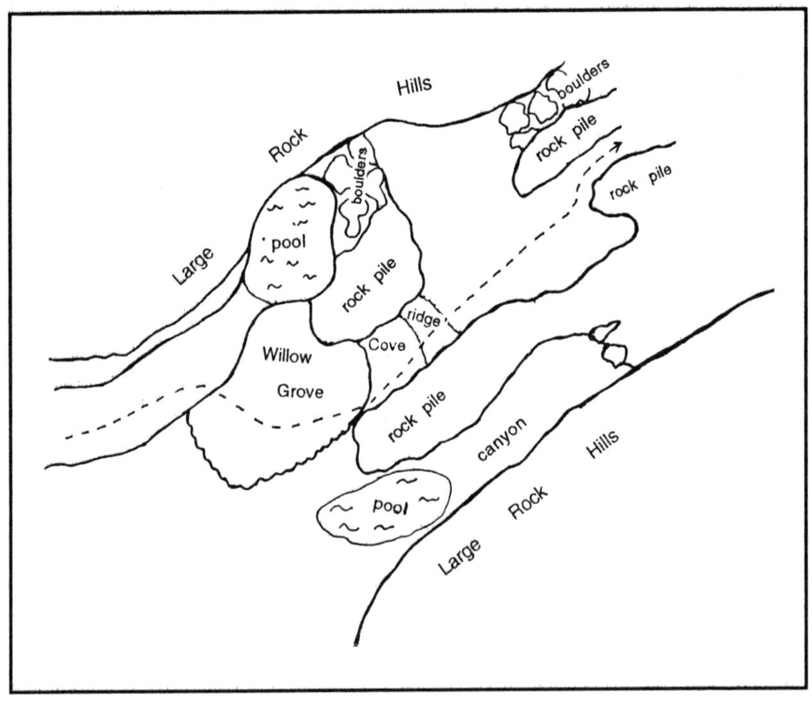


## 5. RATTLESNAKE CANYON - (See Chapter 12, Hike # 5.)

## 6. GUN SIGHT LOOP - (See Chapter 12, Hike # 3.)

# Chapter 17

# COXCOMB MOUNTAINS

The Coxcomb Mountain Range is a wilderness of remote, highly-distinctive, rugged peaks. The area is a sanctuary for desert bighorn sheep which roam at ease, but in limited numbers, through this isolated maze of mountains. (Watch for signs of sheep but avoid disturbing this diminishing species. Refer to Chapter 3, "Understanding Day Use Areas And Desert Bighorn Sheep.") The sandy washes that wind through these mountains aid travel and route-finding; however, proficient map and compass skills are still essential for exploring this towering jumble of rocks.

Access to the Coxcombs is from Pinto Wells, just inside the south boundary of the monument, or from Hwy 62, above the north boundary (39 miles east of Twentynine Palms). There are no campgrounds or towns for miles in any direction. Since there are no backcountry boards, those interested in overnight hikes should inquire and register at Monument Headquarters (Oasis Visitor Center) in Twentynine Palms.

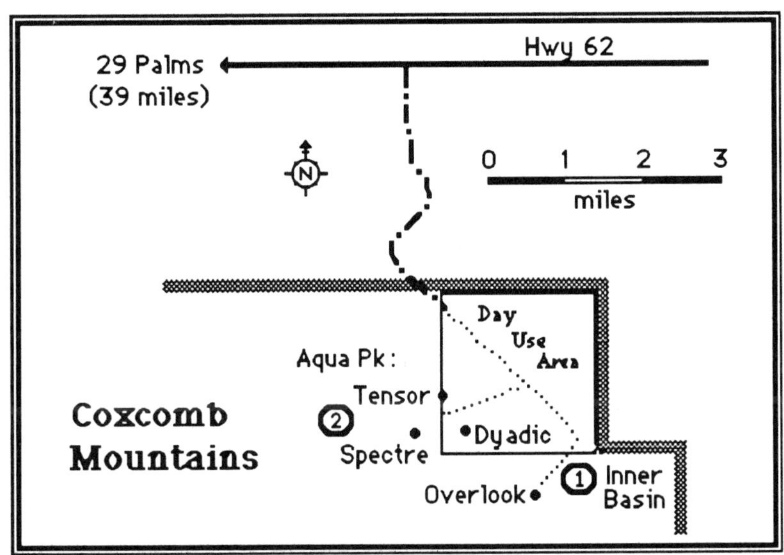

## 1. INNER BASIN

**Type:** x-country, day/overnight (note day use area on map)
**Mileage**: 8 miles
**Time**: 6 hours
**Difficulty**: moderately strenuous, moderately difficult
**Elevation Extremes**: 2700' - 3050' **Difference:** 350'
**Starting and Ending Point:** Coxcomb Parking Area (2700')
**Topo Map**: Cadiz Valley SW 7.5, Cadiz Valley SE 7.5'

Summary: This route provides the easiest access into the Coxcombs. The route travels through washes and along rocky ridges to a basin within the mountains. A trip to the edge of this basin leads to a high overlook of Pinto Basin. Most of the hike to the Inner Basin travels through a day use area; camping is allowed in the southern end of the basin.

Several side trips can be made from the Inner Basin. At the southern end of the basin, a wash heads up into the rocky mountains. This same wash leads southeast down through steep-walled canyons. Yet another hike travels down the overlook to Pinto Basin, around the base of the mountains, and back to the parking area.

Route: From the parking area, scramble southeast up the wash to a pass. Cross the pass, then drop into another wash which continues to lead southeast. Follow this wash down to a wash junction and continue southeast. (The main wash leads down to the NNE.) Travel is now uphill in the wash. This wash leads to the Inner Basin. To reach the overlook, follow the wash out into the basin where it curves SSW then W. Continue traveling SSW (leave the wash) to the edge of the basin and the overlook. (See Map # 10, Appendix D.)

## 2. AQUA PEAK (TENSOR, SPECTRE, DYADIC) 4416'

**Type:** x-country, day/overnight (note day use area on map)
**Mileage**: 6 miles
**Time**: 7 - 8 hours
**Difficulty**: strenuous, difficult (+)
**Elevation Extremes**: 2700' - 4416'(+) **Difference:** 1716'
**Starting and Ending Point:** Coxcomb Parking Area (2700')
**Topo Map**: Cadiz Valley 15' or Cadiz Valley SW 7.5'

Summary: Aqua Peak is used as a collective name for three high peaks located in close proximity. These peaks are the highest in the Coxcomb Mountains. They are the most difficult peaks to climb of all the peaks described in this guide. The peaks - Tensor, Spectre, and Dyadic - were apparently named by climbers in the 1940's. Since then the USGS has

*A hiker on Spectre Peak is rewarded with a bird's-eye view of the Coxcomb Mountains*

installed a benchmark on Tensor, the lowest of the three peaks. The benchmark names the peak "Aqua" and records the elevation as 4416'.

The summit of Tensor is the easiest to reach of the three peaks. Dyadic's summit is the most difficult to attain and is seemingly the highest of the three summits. To reach the top of Dyadic requires short sections of technical climbing (5.1-5.4) near the summit. Attaining the summits of Tensor and Spectre involves difficult boulder scrambling but not technical climbing. All three peaks are reached from a plateau that lies at an elevation of 4080'. The longest and most strenuous part of the hike is the climb up the rocky gully that leads to this plateau. All three peaks have summit registers.

Route: From the parking area, climb southeast up the rocky wash to a pass. Descend to a sandy wash on the other side of the pass. About 1/4 mile from the pass, the wash makes a sharp bend to the left and begins to wind through a narrow canyon. Do not enter the canyon. Depart the wash before the sharp bend and continue heading SE over a ridge. Travel west up the major wash that lies at the bottom of this ridge.

Continue one mile up this steep, rocky wash/gully until it levels out on a plateau. The three peaks are reached from this plateau. Tensor is the rounded peak to the NNE; Spectre is the pointed peak to the SSW; Dyadic is located to the SSE. Dyadic is not readily visible from the plateau but can easily be seen from the slopes of Spectre and Tensor. Dyadic is the rock peak with a tall stake planted on the summit. (See Map # 10, Appendix D.)

# Chapter 18

# CASTLES AND ARCHES

# THE ADVENTURE OF HIKING IN JOSHUA TREE NATIONAL MONUMENT

This final chapter presents a challenge - the challenge to embark on an adventure. The adventure could be the search for a castle, a mysterious place within the monument that has eluded hikers for many years. Or it could be the challenge to locate the monument's largest known arch which has only recently been discovered. Or it could be a self-proclaimed adventure. This chapter is not meant to guide the hiker to another special place. Its purpose is to establish an awareness of the unlimited hiking adventures that exist within Joshua Tree National Monument. Hiking with a guide book is just the beginning.

There are not many people who know about the prospector's castle which lies in a rugged and isolated section of Joshua Tree National Monument. Much of the history surrounding the castle is a mystery. It was occupied by a single man sometime around 1940. It is not known from where this man came or to where he went. The fact that he lived at the site around 1940 is surmised from a collection of dated magazines found in a cave near the castle.

The prospector's self-proclaimed castle is by no means elaborate. In fact, it's not a castle by dictionary definition. In actuality, it is only a small single-room house built under a giant boulder. Mortar and rocks from the desert were used to fill in the gaps between the boulder walls. The house was finished with steps, a hinged door, screen windows, and a chimney. Inside the house, there were all the comforts of home -- a bed, chair, and a table.

The prospector's castle may not be as glamorous as a real castle, but it is more unique. It is an example of how someone can adapt to a harsh desert environment and build a house from raw natural resources. Anyone with money can build a castle, but only a person with determination and a love for the desert can take the resources at hand and make the desert into a pleasing, satisfying home.

Note to castle hikers: Please don't disturb the castle. It remains in excellent condition. (Do not remove "historic litter," i.e. tin cans, magazines.) Allow other hikers to experience this unique, undisturbed site.

*The Castle*

Another adventure may be the quest to find Garrett's Arch. The arch is located deep in the heart of the Wonderland of Rocks and high up in a large rock formation. Blue sky colors the opening beneath the arch. This creates the appearance of a large eye staring from the head of a giant rock monster. From the valley floor, the arch appears dwarfed by the large rock faces that flank both sides of the tunnel opening. However, the vegetation surrounding the arch puts the size of the arch back in perspective. A mature oak tree growing in the opening under the arch only fills up about 1/3 of the opening.

The hike to the arch involves easy traveling. And the arch itself is readily visible from the valley floor. However, the trick to reaching the arch is locating the correct valley. The Wonderland consists of a maze of valleys nestled between large rock formations.

This book has described selective samplings of some of the most interesting and most notable areas with the 560,000 acres of the monument. However, this guide is not meant to provide descriptions and directions to every place of interest within the monument. To do so would take away some of the adventure and mystery that surrounds that which is unknown about this desert wilderness. To be able to hike through a remote area and not know exactly what will be found is exciting. To discover something new while hiking in that area is rewarding. To search for the rumored existence of a special place is an adventure.

The quest to find the prospector's castle or Garrett's Arch is an exciting adventure, but an adventure can be found on any hike within the monument. Everyone who hikes in the desert, either on a described guidebook route or on a self-chosen route, will find something that is new and exciting to them. The desert wilderness holds many secrets and natural wonders that are waiting to be explored or discovered by those who travel **on foot in Joshua Tree National Monument.**

# Appendix A

## LANDMARK DESCRIPTIONS AND DIRECTIONS

Barker Dam Parking Area -- Follow the dirt road east out of Hidden Valley Campground. Turn right at "T" intersection. Take the next road on the left and follow it to the end.

Berdoo Canyon Road -- 4x4 road. Follow the Geology Tour Road 7.7 miles south of PR #12 to a point where the road forks. The right fork is the continuation of GTR, the left fork is the Berdoo Canyon Road.

Black Rock -- Follow Joshua Lane south off Highway 62 in Yucca Valley. Follow the signs to reach the campground, ranger station, and visitor center.

Black Rock Trailhead -- marked by large trailboard to the left (east) of the campground entrance arch

Cap Rock Parking Area -- first parking area on the left (east) side of Keys View Road; 0.2 miles south of Park Route #12 junction

Canyon Road -- leads south from Hwy 62 to the 49 Palms parking area; 4 miles west of Adobe Road in 29 Palms; 1.75 miles east of Indian Cove Road

Chiriaco Summit -- on Interstate 10; 4.5 miles east of Park Route #11

Cottonwood Springs Oasis -- located at the end of the paved spur road that begins just south of Cottonwood Visitor Center; location of the Cottonwood Backcountry Board.

Covington Flats Entrance -- Take La Contenta Road off of Hwy 62, east of Yucca Valley. Follow La Contenta to a junction on the left side of the road (2.8 miles from Hwy 62). Turn left and continue 1.7 miles to the monument boundary.

Covington Flats Backcountry Board -- Turn right at the junction located 4.2 miles southeast of Covington Entrance. Travel to a "T" intersection, turn left, and follow the road to the end.

Covington Flats Picnic Area -- From Covington Flats Entrance, continue southeast to the end of the road.

Coxcomb Parking Area -- Drive east on Hwy 62 approximately 39 miles from Utah Trail. Turn right at low point in road. Follow a dirt road/wash 4.4 miles to its end at the base of a rocky gully.

Echo "T" Intersection -- Follow the dirt road east out of Hidden Valley Campground to a "T" intersection.

Eureka Peak Parking -- Turn right at the junction 4.2 miles south of Covington Entrance. Travel to a "T" intersection, turn right, and follow the road to the west end of Upper Covington Flats.

Fried Liver Wash, PR #11 -- mile wide wash that crosses Park Route #11 near mile 13

Geology Tour Road (GTR) -- heads south off of Park Route #12; 5 miles west of Pinto Wye; 2.4 miles east of Sheep Pass.

Geology Tour Backcountry Board -- on left side of GTR; 1.4 miles south of Park Route #12 junction

Hidden Valley Campground -- on Park Route #12; 4.5 miles west of Sheep Pass; 8.7 miles east of the West Entrance

Hidden Valley Picnic Area -- south side of Park Route #12 across from Hidden Valley Campground

Indian Cove Road -- leads south off of Hwy 62; 5.7 miles west of Adobe Road in 29 Palms; 9 miles east of Park Blvd in Joshua Tree; leads to a ranger station, picnic area, and campground

Indian Cove Backcountry Board -- on the right (west) side of Indian Cove Road; 0.4 miles south of the Indian Cove Ranger Station

Indian Cove Picnic Area -- far left (east) end of Indian Cove Campground

Jumbo Rocks Campground -- on Park Route #12; 3.4 miles west of Pinto Wye; 4 miles east of Sheep Pass

Juniper Flats Backcountry Board -- on right (west) side of Keys View Road; one mile south of Park Route #12 junction

Keys View -- end of Keys View Road (Park Route #13)

Keys West Gate Backcountry Board -- located at a bend in Park Route #12; 2.3 miles west of Hidden Valley Campground; 6.4 miles from the West Entrance.

Live Oak Picnic Area -- on the south side of Park Route #12; 2 miles west of Pinto Wye; 5.3 miles east of Sheep Pass

Lost Horse Mine Parking -- Follow Keys View Road (PR#13) south 2.4 miles. Turn left (east) onto dirt road and follow it to the end.

Lucky Boy Junction -- A dirt road leads north off of Park Route #12 opposite the Geology Tour Road. Follow the dirt road north about one mile to the junction of a gated east leading road.

Mt. San Gorgonio -- prominent peak (11,499') located west of monument

Mt. San Jacinto -- prominent peak (10,804') located south of monument

North Entrance -- end of Utah Trail; 4 miles south of Hwy 62

North Entrance Exhibit -- located 0.5 miles south of the North Entrance on the west side of the road.

North Entrance Backcountry Board -- on east side of Park Route #12 at the end of a short dirt road; 0.5 miles south of the North Entrance

Oasis Visitor Center -- main visitor center located at monument headquarters on Utah Trail in 29 Palms

O'Dell Road Parking Area -- Follow the dirt road east out of Hidden Valley Campground. Turn right at "T" intersection. Follow road 1.7

miles to a three fork intersection. Take the middle fork. Continue 1.5 miles to a junction. Turn left (north). Follow the road to the end.

Park Route #11 -- main north/south road between Pinto Wye and I-10

Park Route #12 -- main east/west road between the North Entrance and West Entrance

Park Route #13 (Keys View Road) -- heads south off of Park Route #12; 7.4 miles west of Sheep Pass; 10.4 miles east of West Entrance

Pine City Backcountry Board -- A dirt road heads north off PR #12 opposite the Geology Tour Road. Follow it to the end (1.2 miles).

Pinkham Road -- heads west off Park Route #11 near the Cottonwood Visitor Center; rough four-wheel drive dirt road

Pinto Wye -- junction of Park Route #12 and Park Route #11; 4.6 miles south of the North Entrance; 35.7 miles north of the South Entrance and 20.6 miles east of the West Entrance

Pinyon Well Parking Area -- southwest corner of one-way loop on Geology Tour Road; 9.5 miles from Park Route #12; stop #15 GTR

Pleasant Valley Backcountry Board -- at end of first leg of one-way loop on Geology Tour Road; 6.8 miles from Park Route #12

Porcupine Wash Backcountry Board -- west side of PR #11; 21.3 miles south of Pinto Wye; 8.4 miles north of Cottonwood Visitor Center

Quail Springs Picnic Area -- south side of Park Route #12; 3 miles west of Hidden Valley Campground; 5.8 miles east of the West Entrance

Radio Tower Road -- Head west off Joshua Lane onto San Andreas Road. At the end of the paved road, take the right fork of the dirt road. Follow the road along the power lines 0.6 miles then turn left (south). Travel 0.6 miles to a major road fork. Travel to the right and go another 0.3 miles to another fork. Travel to the left. Radio Tower Road junction is about 1.3 miles beyond the second fork. The tower is visible at this junction. Travel 1/2 mile southwest up Radio Tower Road. Just below the tower, there is a sharp bend with a rock/cement drainage ditch on the left side. At this point, there is a gully on the left side of the road which leads down to Long Canyon. (Although these dirt roads may be rough, four-wheel drive is usually not necessary.)

Ryan Campground -- on Park Route #12; 2.3 miles west of Sheep Pass; 11 miles east of the West Entrance

Ryan Mountain Parking Area -- south side of Park Route #12; 0.7 miles west of Sheep Pass; 12.5 miles east of the West Entrance

Santa Rosa Mtns. -- distant mountain range located south of the monument and south of Coachella Valley

Sheep Pass -- on Park Route #12; 12 miles from the North Entrance; 13.2 miles from the West Entrance; group campground; road pass

South Park Parking Area -- Follow the short dirt road that leads west immediately before the entrance to Black Rock Campground. Travel the road to the end.

Split Rock Picnic Area -- on north side of Park Route #12; 2 miles west of Pinto Wye; 6 miles east of Sheep Pass

Squaw Tank -- stop # 9 on Geology Tour Road; 5.3 miles from Park Route #12 junction

Stop # 7 -- on Geology Tour Road; 4.6 miles south of PR #12 junction

Stop # 14 -- on Geology Tour Road; 9.5 miles from PR #12 junction

Turkey Flats Backcountry Board -- on east side of PR #11; 16.2 miles south of Pinto Wye; 13.5 miles north of Cottonwood Visitor Center

Twin Tanks Backcountry Board -- on west side of PR#11; 2.2 miles south of Pinto Wye; 27.5 miles north of Cottonwood Visitor Center

Utah Trail -- entrance road to monument; leads south off Hwy 62 at east end of Twentynine Palms; passes Monument Headquarters

West Entrance -- end of Park Blvd; 5 miles south of the town of Joshua Tree

West Entrance Wash -- 1.2 miles east of the West Entrance. There's a pullout on the north side of the road adjacent to the wash.

White Tank Campground -- on Park Route #11; 2.7 miles south of Pinto Wye; 27 miles north of Cottonwood Visitor Center

Wonderland Ranch Parking -- Follow the dirt road east out of Hidden Valley Campground. Turn right at the "T" intersection. Travel one mile. Take the second left and follow the road to the end.

# Appendix B

## GLOSSARY Of Common Terms and Abbreviations

alluvial fan -- large sloping areas at the base of mountains. The slopes were formed by deposited sediments which were carried out of the mountains with rainwater run-off.

arrastra -- drag stone mill used for crushing ore

b/c -- backcountry board; place to register for overnight hikes

bedrock mortar -- a hole in a rock in which Indians ground seeds

cairn -- pile of rocks or stones used as a trail marker or summit marker

class III climbing -- difficult scrambling over rocks; hands and feet used to ascend. A rope is sometimes desired.

class IV climbing -- actual climbing up rocks with use of hands and feet. A rope is used for inexperienced climbers.

desert varnish -- dark mineral stain on rocks

GTR -- Geology Tour Road; Chapter 9

inholding -- private property within the monument boundaries

petroglyph -- rock carvings made by the early Indians. The carved symbols may have been a form of writing or perhaps just doodlings.

QSPA -- Quail Springs Picnic Area

slot canyon -- narrow canyon between solid rock cliffs

tailings -- crushed rocks that surround the entrance to many mine shafts.

tank -- water-catch basin formed by a low dam spanning the width of a wash. Most of the tanks in the monument are filled with sand.

wash -- drainages and water paths which are dry except during rainstorms. Most desert washes are sandy.

x/c -- x-country; traveling through the desert without the use of man-made travel aids

# Appendix C

# PEAK BAGGER'S GUIDE,

# MILEAGE CHART, EXTENDED TRIPS

## Peak Bagger's Guide

| Peak | Elevation | Elevation Gain | Hike Reference |
|---|---|---|---|
| Quail Mountain | 5813' | 2133' | Chap. 7, Hike # 3 |
| | | 1473' | Chap. 10, Hike # 3 |
| Queen Mountain | 5687' | 1207' | Chap. 8, Hike # 3 |
| Inspiration Peak | 5558' | 408' | Chap. 10, Hike # 9 |
| Eureka Peak | 5518' | 1538' | Chap. 13, Hike # 6 |
| Ryan Mountain | 5457' | 977' | Chap. 7, Hike # 8 |
| Little Berdoo Peak | 5440' | 2190' | Chap. 9, Hike # 8 |
| Bernard Peak | 5430' | 2180' | Chap. 9, Hike # 8 |
| Eagle Peak | 5350' | 2350' | Chap. 15, Hike # 4 |
| Lost Horse Mtn. | 5313' | 713' | Chap. 10, Hike # 6 |
| Warren Peak | 5103' | 1123' | Chap. 13, Hike # 4 |
| Negro Hill | 4875' | 439' | Chap. 8, Hike # 4 |
| Monument Mtn. | 4834' | 2434' | Chap. 14, Hike # 11 |
| | | 1594' | Chap. 15, Hike # 1 |
| Lela Peak | 4747' | 1227' | Chap. 9, Hike # 3 |
| Crown Prince | 4581' | 181' | Chap. 6, Hike # 9 |
| Aqua Peak | 4416' | 1716' | Chap. 17, Hike # 2 |
| South Park Peak | 4395' | 255' | Chap. 13, Hike # 2 |
| Malapai Hill | 4280' | 520' | Chap. 9, Hike # 2 |
| Pinto Mountain | 3983' | 2383' | Chap. 14, Hike # 9 |
| Mary Peak | 3820' | 2064' | Chap. 14, Hike # 7 |
| Joshua Mountain | 3746' | 1176' | Chap. 6, Hike # 2 |
| Mastodon Peak | 3440' | 440' | Chap. 15, Hike # 6 |

# Mileage Chart

| Easy Hikes | Miles | Hours | Chapter # | | Hike # |
|---|---|---|---|---|---|
| Cholla Cactus Garden | 0.25 | <1 | 5. | Nature Trail | 10 |
| Keys View | 0.25 | <1 | 5. | Nature Trail | 5 |
| Arch Rock | 0.3 | <1 | 5. | Nature Trail | 9 |
| Cap Rock | 0.4 | <1 | 5. | Nature Trail | 4 |
| Oasis of Mara | 0.5 | <1 | 5. | Nature Trail | 8 |
| Indian Cove | 0.6 | <1 | 5. | Nature Trail | 7 |
| Live Oak/Ivanpah | 1 | <1 | 6. | PR#12 East | 6 |
| Cottonwood | 1 | 1 | 5. | Nature Trail | 11 |
| Hidden Valley | 1 | 1 | 5. | Nature Trail | 2 |
| Morton's Mill Site | 1 | 1 | 15. | Cottonwood | 5 |
| Barker Dam | 1 | 1 | 5. | Nature Trail | 3 |
| Desert Queen Mine | 1.2 | 1 | 8. | Queen Valley | 7 |
| Wall Street Mill | 1.5 | 1 | 8. | Queen Valley | 2 |
| Skull Rock | 1.7 | 1 | 5. | Nature Trail | 6 |
| Sand Dunes | 2 | 1 | 14. | PR#11 | 8 |
| Wonderland Ranch Wash | 2 | 1.5 | 16. | Wonderland | 2 |
| Lucky Boy Vista | 2.5 | 2 | 8. | Queen Valley | 10 |
| Big Barker Dam Loop | 3 | 2 | 8. | Queen Valley | 1 |
| Pine City | 3 | 2 | 8. | Queen Valley | 5 |
| R&H: GTR - PR#11 (•) | 4.4 | 2-3 | 11. | CA R&H Tr. | 4 |
| Pleasant Valley Road-Trail | 5 | 2-3 | 9. | Geology Tour | 4 |
| Black Rock Canyon | 5 | 2-3 | 13. | Black Rock | 3 |
| R&H: PR#13 - GTR (•) | 6.5 | 3-4 | 11. | CA R&H Tr. | 3 |
| R&H: PR#11 - N. Entrance (•) | 7 | 3-4 | 11. | CA R&H Tr. | 5 |
| Willow Hole | 7 | 4 | 16. | Wonderland | 3 |
| Quail Springs | 7.8 | 4 | 7. | PR#12 West | 1 |
| Quail Springs Road/Wash (•) | 8.5 | 5 | 7. | PR#12 West | 1 |
| Juniper Flats | 9 | 4-6 | 10. | Keys View | 2 |
| Eagle Mt. Road-Trail | 11 | 5-6 | 15. | Cottonwood | 3 |
| Fried Liver Wash (•) | 14 | 7-9 | 9. | Geology Tour | 7 |

| Moderate Hikes | Miles | Hours | Chapter # | | Hike # |
|---|---|---|---|---|---|
| South Park Peak | 0.8 | 1 | 13. | Black Rock | 2 |
| Sneakeye Spring | 1 | 1 | 12. | Indian Cove | 4 |
| Silver Bell Mine | 1 | 1 | 14. | PR#11 | 4 |
| High View | 1.3 | 1 | 5. | Nature Trail | 1 |
| Grand Tank (~) | 1.25 | 1 | 14. | PR#11 | 1 |
| Twin Tanks | 2 | 1-2 | 14. | PR#11 | 2 |

| Moderate Hikes (cont.) | Miles | Hours | Chapter # | Hike # |
|---|---|---|---|---|
| Mastodon Loop | 3 | 2 | 15. Cottonwood | 6 |
| Crown Prince Lookout (~) | 3 | 2 | 6. PR#12 East | 9 |
| Desert Queen Wash (•*) | 3.5 | 2-3 | 8. Queen Valley | 8 |
| Lost Horse Mine | 4 | 2-3 | 10. Keys View | 5 |
| Eldorado Mine | 4 | 2-3 | 14. PR#11 | 4 |
| Pine City Canyon (•**) | 5.5 | 4 | 8. Queen Valley | 6 |
| Covington Loop | 5.7 | 3-4 | 13. Black Rock | 8 |
| Black Rock - Covington (•) | 7.5 | 3-5 | 11. CA R&H Tr. | 1 |
| Eldorado Mine (•) | 7.5 | 4-5 | 9. Geology Tour | 6 |
| Lost Palms Oasis | 7.5 | 4-6 | 15. Cottonwood | 7 |
| Boy Scout Trail (•) | 8 | 4-5 | 7. PR#12 West | 5 |
| Porcupine/Ruby Lee | 8.5 | 5-6 | 14. PR#11 | 10 |
| Smith Water Canyon (•**) | 8.5 | 5-7 | 13. Black Rock | 7 |
| Long Canyon / Chuckawalla | 10 | 6 | 13. Black Rock | 5 |
| Johnny Lang Canyon (~) | 10.5 | 6-7 | 7. PR#12 West | 4 |
| Eldorado Mine | 11 | 6-7 | 9. Geology Tour | 6 |

| Moderately Strenuous Hikes | Miles | Hours | Chapter # | Hike # |
|---|---|---|---|---|
| Pinto Wye Arrastra | 1.25 | 1 | 6. PR#12 East | 5 |
| Negro Hill | 1.5 | 1.5 | 8. Queen Valley | 4 |
| Malapai Hill (*) | 1.5 | 1-2 | 9. Geology Tour | 2 |
| Inspiration Peak (~) | 1.5 | 1.5 | 10. Keys View | 9 |
| Pinto Wye Arrastra Loop (**) | 2 | 1.5 | 6. PR#12 East | 5 |
| 49 Palms Oasis | 3 | 2-3 | 12. Indian Cove | 6 |
| Ryan Mountain | 3 | 2-3 | 7. PR#12 West | 8 |
| Contact Mine | 3.4 | 2-3 | 6. PR#12 East | 3 |
| Golden Bee Mine | 3.5 | 2-3 | 14. PR#11 | 4 |
| Lost Horse Mountain | 4.5 | 3 | 10. Keys View | 6 |
| Eureka Peak (•) | 5 | 3-4 | 13. Black Rock | 6 |
| Warren Peak (~) | 6 | 3-4 | 13. Black Rock | 4 |
| Pushawalla Plateau | 6.5 | 4-5 | 9. Geology Tour | 9 |
| Johnny Lang Viewpoint | 7.5 | 4-5 | 7. PR#12 West | 4 |
| Hexahedron Mine | 8 | 5-6 | 9. Geology Tour | 5 |
| Inner Basin (*) | 8 | 6 | 17. Coxcomb | 1 |
| Lost Horse Loop | 8.4 | 5-6 | 10. Keys View | 7 |
| R&H: Covington - PR#13 (•) | 10 | 5-7 | 11. CA R&H Tr. | 2 |
| Blue Cut Loop | 14.5 | 8-10 | 9. Geology Tour | 10 |

| Strenuous Hikes | Miles | Hours | Chapter # | | Hike # |
|---|---|---|---|---|---|
| Eagle Cliff Hills/Mine (*) | 2.5 | 2-3 | 6. | PR#12 East | 8 |
| Joshua Mountain (**) | 2.6 | 2-3 | 6. | PR#12 East | 2 |
| Gun Sight Loop (***) | 2.75 | 4 | 12. | Indian Cove | 3 |
| Rattlesnake Canyon (**) | 3 | 3 | 12. | Indian Cove | 5 |
| Queen Mountain (*) | 4 | 3-4 | 8. | Queen Valley | 3 |
| Eagle Cliff Mine (*) | 4.5 | 3-4 | 8. | Queen Valley | 9 |
| Lela Peak | 5 | 3-4 | 9. | Geology Tour | 3 |
| Wonderland Connection (•***) | 5.5 | 6 | 16. | Wonderland | 4 |
| Monument Mtn (*) | 6 | 5-6 | 15. | Cottonwood | 1 |
| Aqua Peak (***) | 6 | 7-8 | 17. | Coxcombs | 2 |
| Mary Peak | 6.5 | 4-6 | 14. | PR#11 | 7 |
| Bernard/Berdoo Mts, Nard (*) | 6.5 | 5-7 | 9. | Geology Tour | 8 |
| 49 Palms Canyon (***) | 8 | 6-9 | 12. | Indian Cove | 7 |
| Bernard/Berdoo Mts, Rt.#1 (*) | 8.5 | 6-7 | 9. | Geology Tour | 8 |
| Johnny Lang Mine | 9 | 6-7 | 7. | PR#12 West | 4 |
| Pinto Mountain, S Wash (**) | 9 | 7-9 | 14. | PR#11 | 9 |
| Munsen Canyon (**) | 9 | 7-10 | 15. | Cottonwood | 8 |
| Eagle Peak (**) | 10 | 8-10 | 15. | Cottonwood | 4 |
| Bernard/Berdoo Mts, Rt.#2 (*) | 11.5 | 6-8 | 9. | Geology Tour | 8 |
| Munsen Canyon (**) | 12 | 9-12 | 15. | Cottonwood | 8 |
| Quail Mountain | 12 | 6-8 | 10. | Keys View | 3 |
| Quail Mountain (**) | 12 | 7-9 | 7. | PR#12 West | 3 |
| Pinto Mountain, W. Wash (**) | 12 | 8-10 | 14. | PR#11 | 9 |
| Pinto Mountain, SE Wash (*) | 13 | 8-10 | 14. | PR#11 | 9 |
| Monument Mtn (*) | 20 | 12-14 | 14. | PR#11 | 11 |

(•) one way hike requiring vehicle shuttle
(~) short section of easy to moderate scrambling
(*) moderately difficult scrambling
(**) difficult scrambling and boulder hopping
(***) extra-difficult scrambling, bouldering, climbing

## Extended Backpack Trips

Although the longest hike described in this guide is only 20 miles, the possibilities for planning extended backpack trips are limited only by the imagination. Days may be spent traveling through the monument from the east to the west or from the north to the south. Here are a few ideas for some extended trips which involve combining several hikes described in the guide. (Numbers denote hike numbers, i.e. 5:4 is Chapter 5, Hike # 4.

Keys Gate Loop — 22.7 miles

Keys West Gate to QSPA; up Quail Mountain via north wash (7:3); down Quail Mountain via southeast ridge to Juniper Flats (10:3); R&H trail west to Covington (11:2); Smith Water Canyon to QSPA (13:7) to Keys West Gate.

Black Rock to Indian Cove — 24.6 miles

R&H -- Black Rock to Covington (11:1); Smith Water Canyon to QSPA (13:7); QSPA to Keys Gate; Boy Scout Trail to Indian Cove (7:5).

Riding & Hiking trail from Black Rock to North Entrance — 35.4 miles

Indian Cove Loop — 38.7 miles

Indian Cove to Keys West Gate via Boy Scout Trail (7:5); Keys Gate Loop (above); Indian Cove via the Boy Scout Trail (7:5).

# Appendix D
# TOPOGRAPHICAL MAPS

*Map # 1 - USGS topographical map: Joshua Tree 15' (1955)*

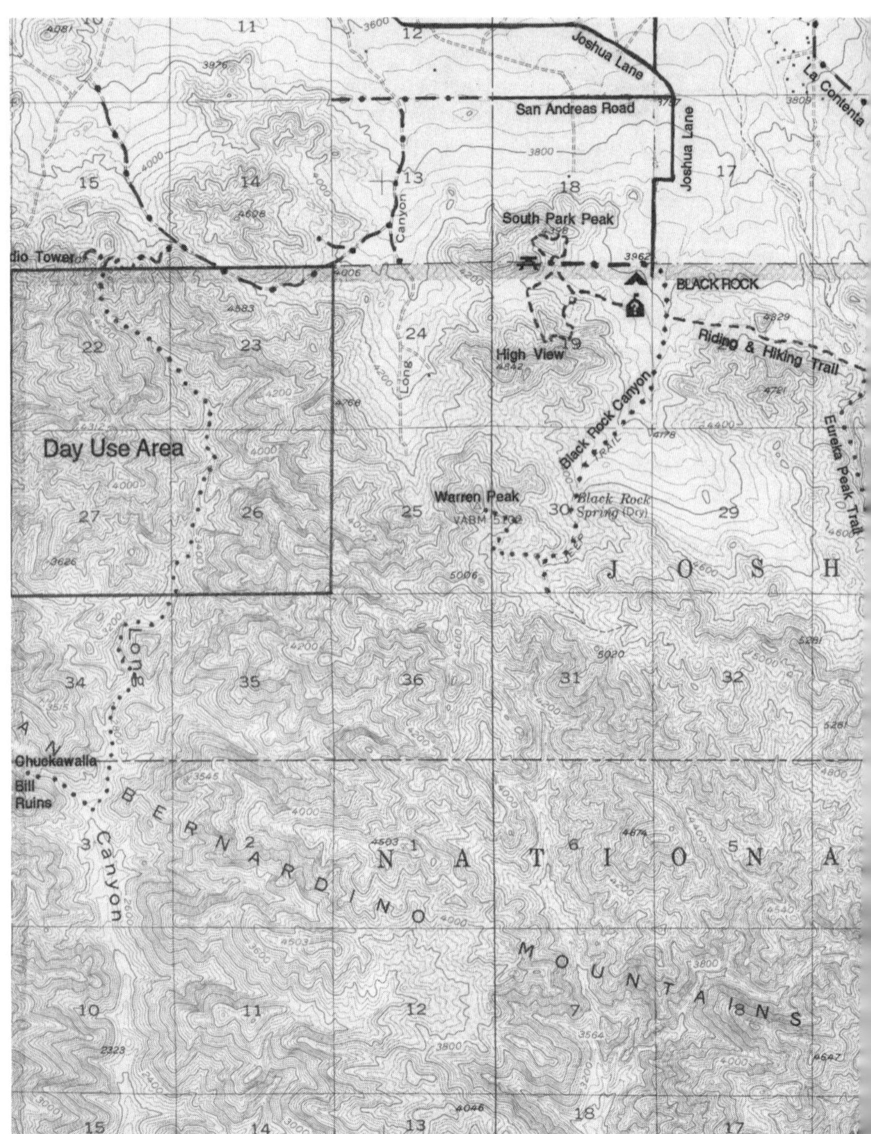

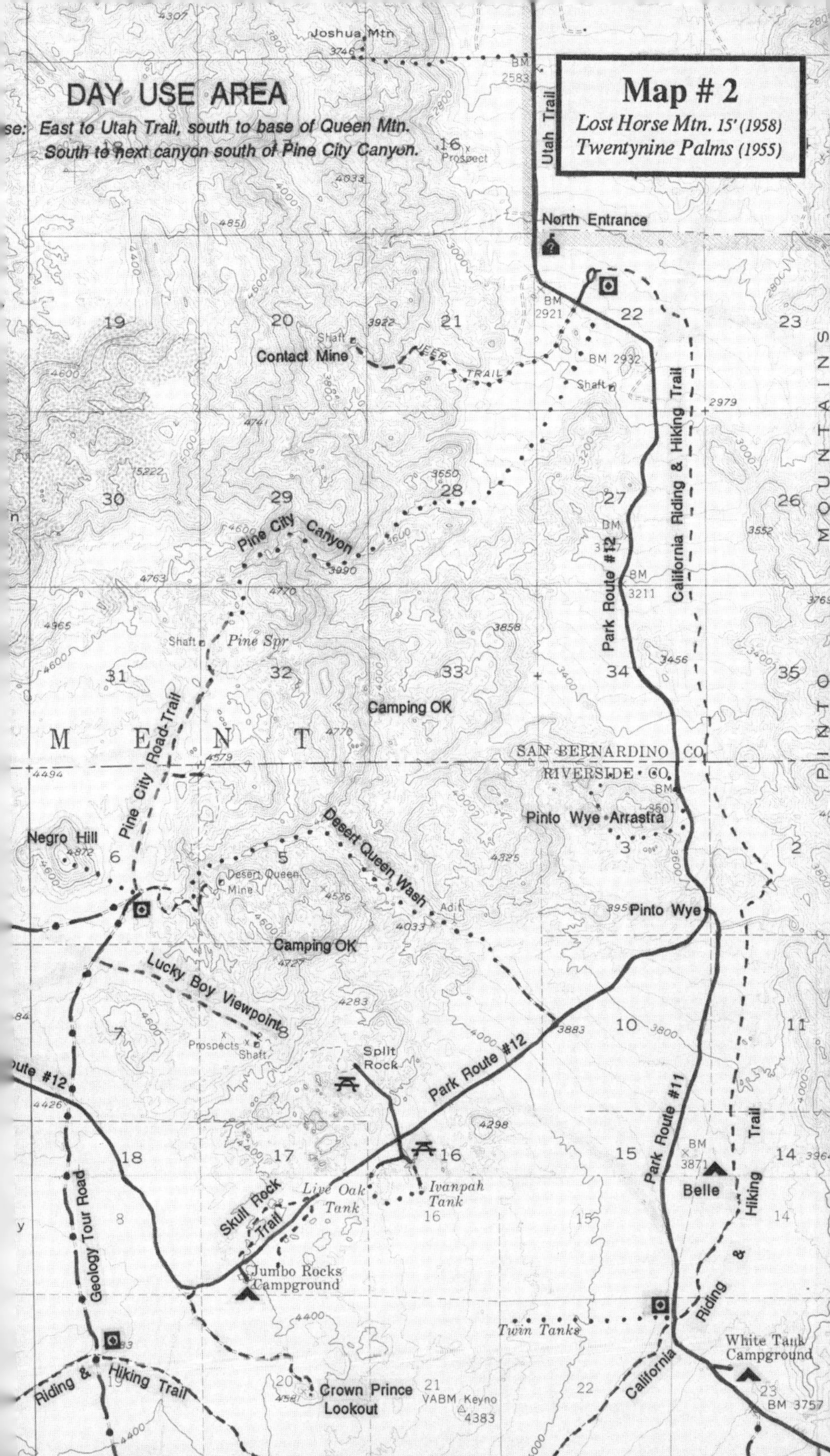
Map # 2
Lost Horse Mtn. 15' (1958)
Twentynine Palms (1955)
DAY USE AREA
se: East to Utah Trail, south to base of Queen Mtn.
South to next canyon south of Pine City Canyon.
Joshua Mtn
Utah Trail
North Entrance
Contact Mine
Jeep Trail
Pine City Canyon
Pine Spr
Camping OK
California Riding & Hiking Trail
Park Route #12
SAN BERNARDINO CO
RIVERSIDE CO
Pinto Wye Arrastra
Pinto Wye
Pine City Road-Trail
Negro Hill
Desert Queen Mine
Desert Queen Wash
Camping OK
Lucky Boy Viewpoint
Prospects
Split Rock
Park Route #12
Park Route #11
Riding & Hiking Trail
Belle
Skull Rock Trail
Live Oak Tank
Ivanpah Tank
Jumbo Rocks Campground
Geology Tour Road
Twin Tanks
White Tank Campground
California Riding
Riding & Hiking Trail
Crown Prince Lookout
VABM Keyno
PINTO MOUNTAINS

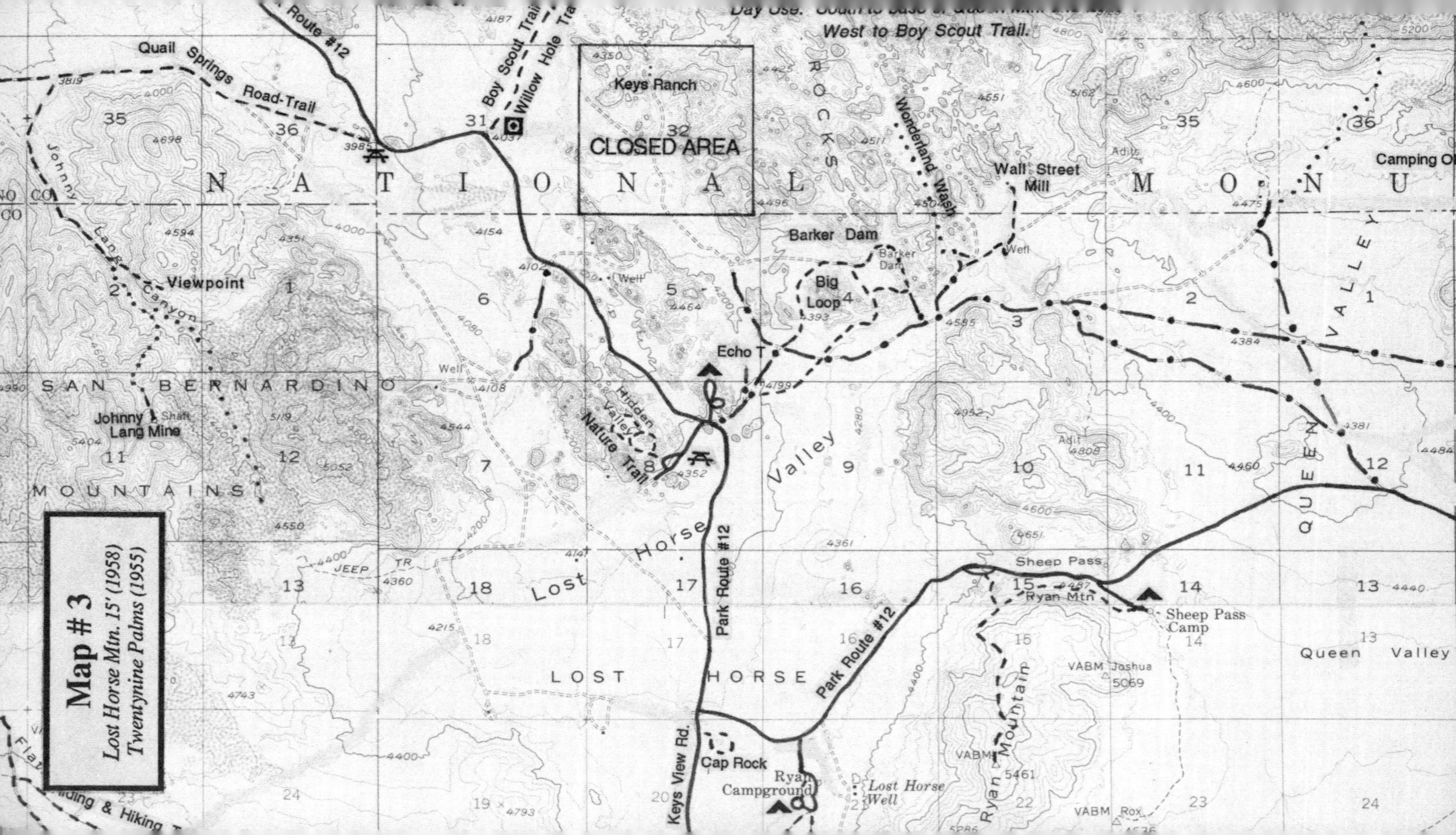

Map # 3
Lost Horse Mtn. 15' (1958)
Twentynine Palms (1955)
West to Boy Scout Trail.
Route #12
Quail Springs Road-Trail
Boy Scout Trail
Willow Hole Tra
Keys Ranch
CLOSED AREA
NATIONAL MONU
ROCKS
Wonderland Wash
Wall Street Mill
Camping OK
Barker Dam
Big Loop 4
Johnny Lang Canyon
Viewpoint
SAN BERNARDINO MOUNTAINS
Johnny Lang Mine
Shaft
Echo T
Hidden Valley
Nature Trail
Valley
Lost Horse
Park Route #12
JEEP TR
LOST HORSE
Sheep Pass
Ryan Mtn
Sheep Pass Camp
Queen Valley
QUEEN VALLEY
VABM Joshua 5069
Ryan Mountain
Keys View Rd.
Cap Rock
Ryan Campground
Lost Horse Well
Riding & Hiking

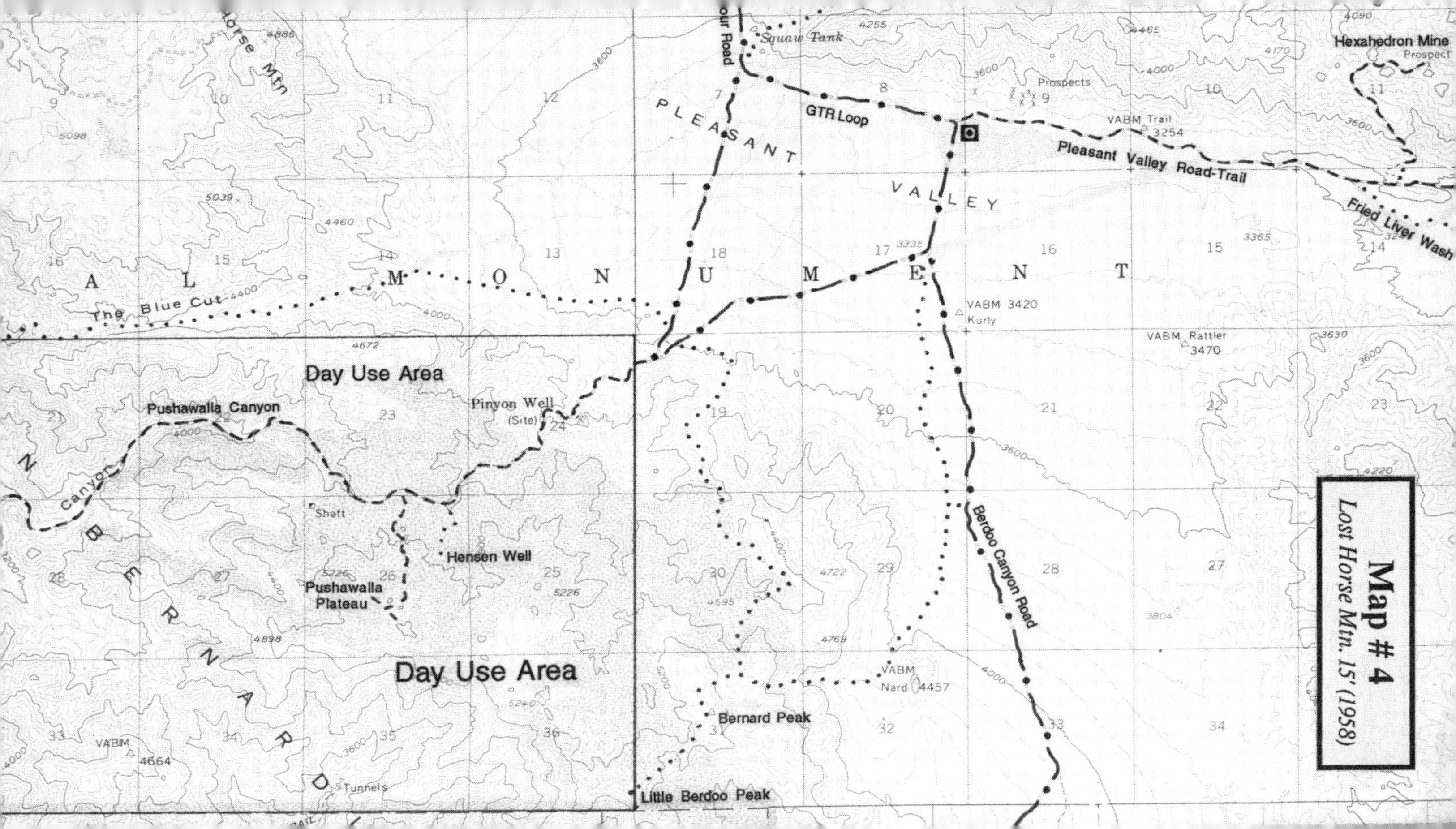

Map # 4
Lost Horse Mtn. 15' (1958)
Hexahedron Mine
Prospect
Prospects
Squaw Tank
GTR Loop
Pleasant Valley Road-Trail
Fried Liver Wash
PLEASANT VALLEY
VABM Trail 3254
VABM 3420 Kurly
VABM Rattler 3470
ALMONUMENT
The Blue Cut
Berdoo Canyon Road
Day Use Area
Pinyon Well (Site)
Pushawalla Canyon
Shaft
Hensen Well
Pushawalla Plateau
Day Use Area
VABM Nard 4457
Bernard Peak
Little Berdoo Peak
Tunnels
VABM 4664
NBERNARD
Canyon

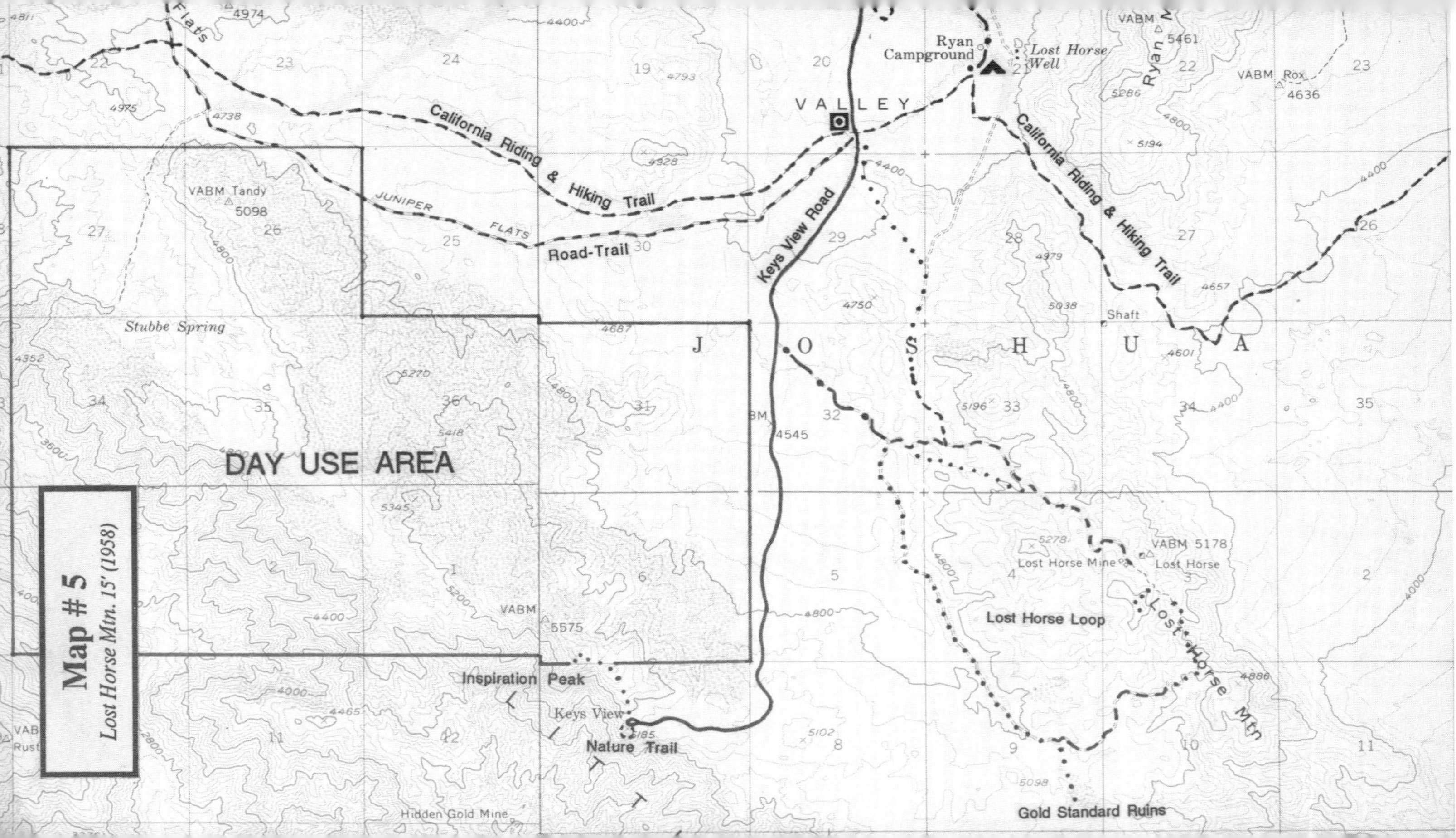

Map # 5
Lost Horse Mtn. 15' (1958)
Flats
Ryan Campground
Lost Horse Well
VABM
Ryan
5461
VABM Rox
4636
VALLEY
California Riding & Hiking Trail
VABM Tandy
5098
JUNIPER FLATS
Road-Trail
Keys View Road
Stubbe Spring
Shaft
J O S H U A
DAY USE AREA
VABM
5575
VABM 5178
Lost Horse Mine
Lost Horse
Lost Horse Loop
Lost Horse Mtn
Inspiration Peak
Keys View
Nature Trail
Hidden Gold Mine
Gold Standard Ruins

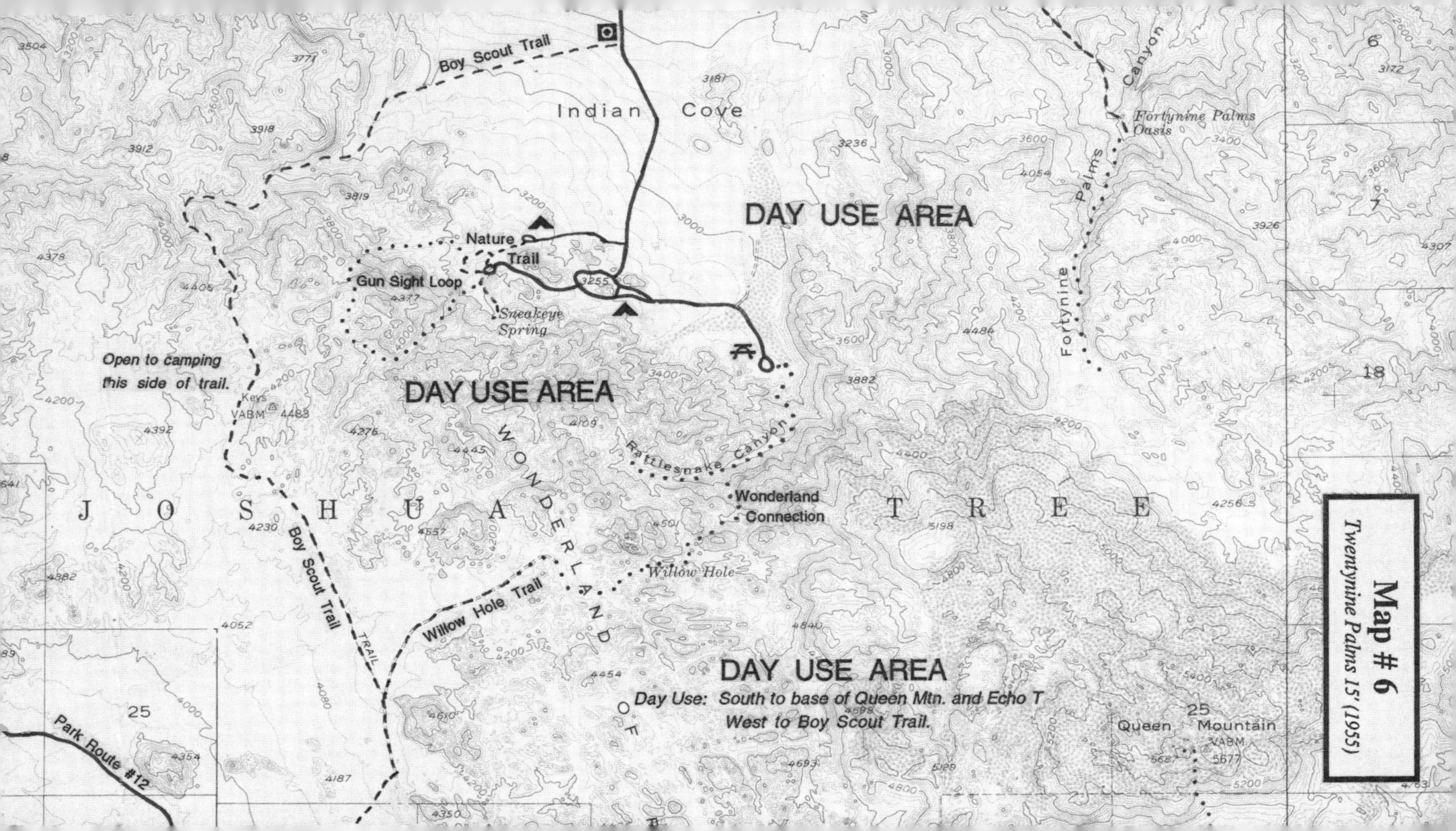

Map # 6
Twentynine Palms 15' (1955)
DAY USE AREA
DAY USE AREA
DAY USE AREA
Day Use: South to base of Queen Mtn. and Echo T
West to Boy Scout Trail.
Open to camping
this side of trail.
Indian Cove
Fortynine Palms
Fortynine Palms Oasis
Canyon
Queen Mountain
Wonderland
Connection
Rattlesnake Canyon
Willow Hole
Willow Hole Trail
Nature
Trail
Sneakeye Spring
Gun Sight Loop
Boy Scout Trail
Boy Scout Trail
TRAIL
Park Route #12
J O S H U A T R E E
W O N D E R L A N D O F
Keys VABM 4483

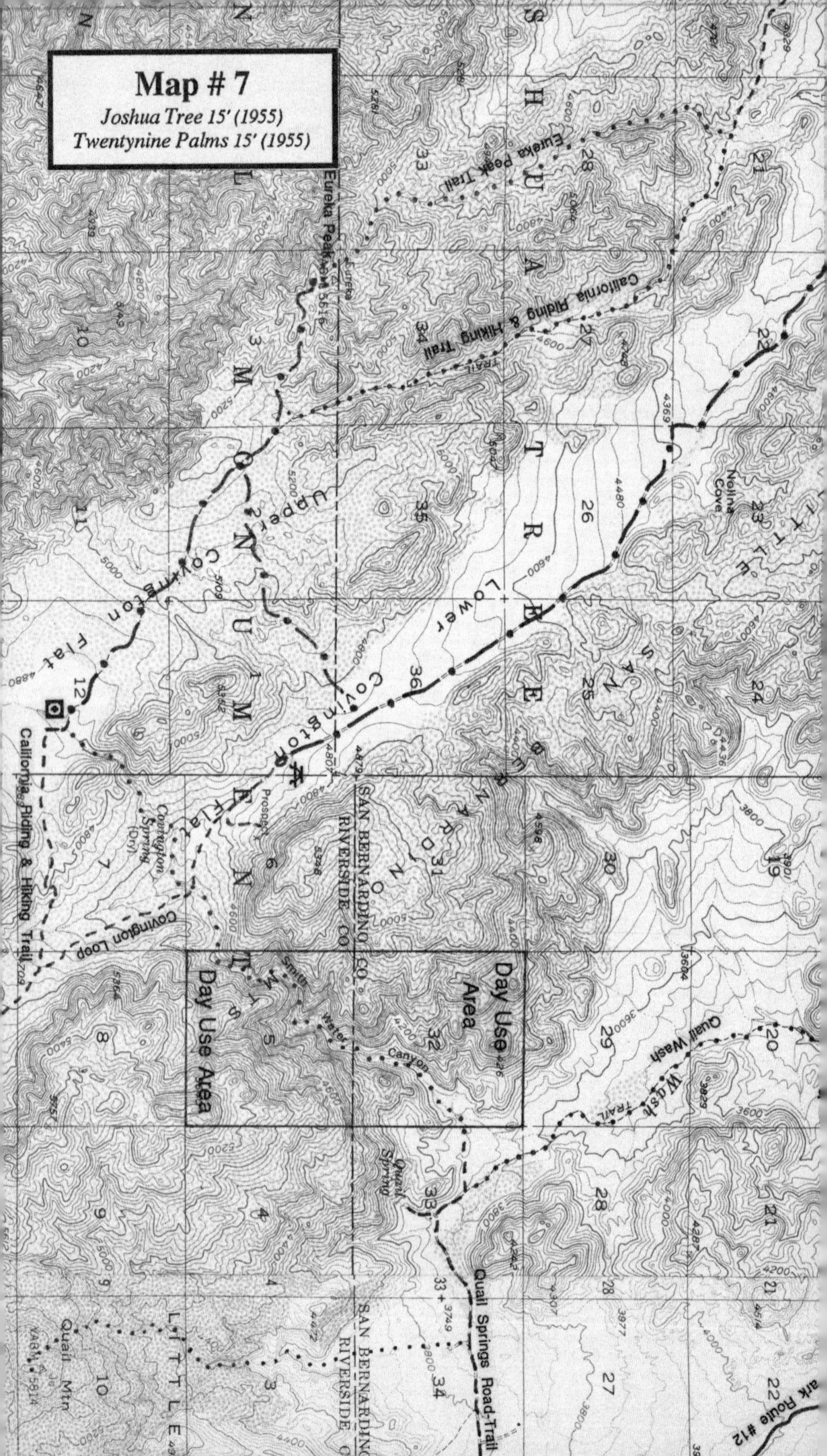

Map # 7
Joshua Tree 15' (1955)
Twentynine Palms 15' (1955)
Eureka Peak Trail
Eureka Peak
California Riding & Hiking Trail
Upper Covington Flat
Lower Covington
Covington Flat
Nolina Cove
San Bernardino Co.
Riverside Co.
Covington Spring (Dry)
Covington Loop
Prospect
Smith Water Canyon
Day Use Area
Quail Wash
Quail Spring
Quail Springs Road-Trail
Quail Mtn

Map # 8
Hexie Mountains 15' (1963)
Park Route #11
Park Route #11
Ruby Lee Mill
Ruby Lee Well
JEEP TRAIL
Porcupine Wash
Wash
Smoke Tree Well
Smoke Tree
Pinkham Road
Pinkham Road
Monument Mtn
PINTO BASIN ROAD

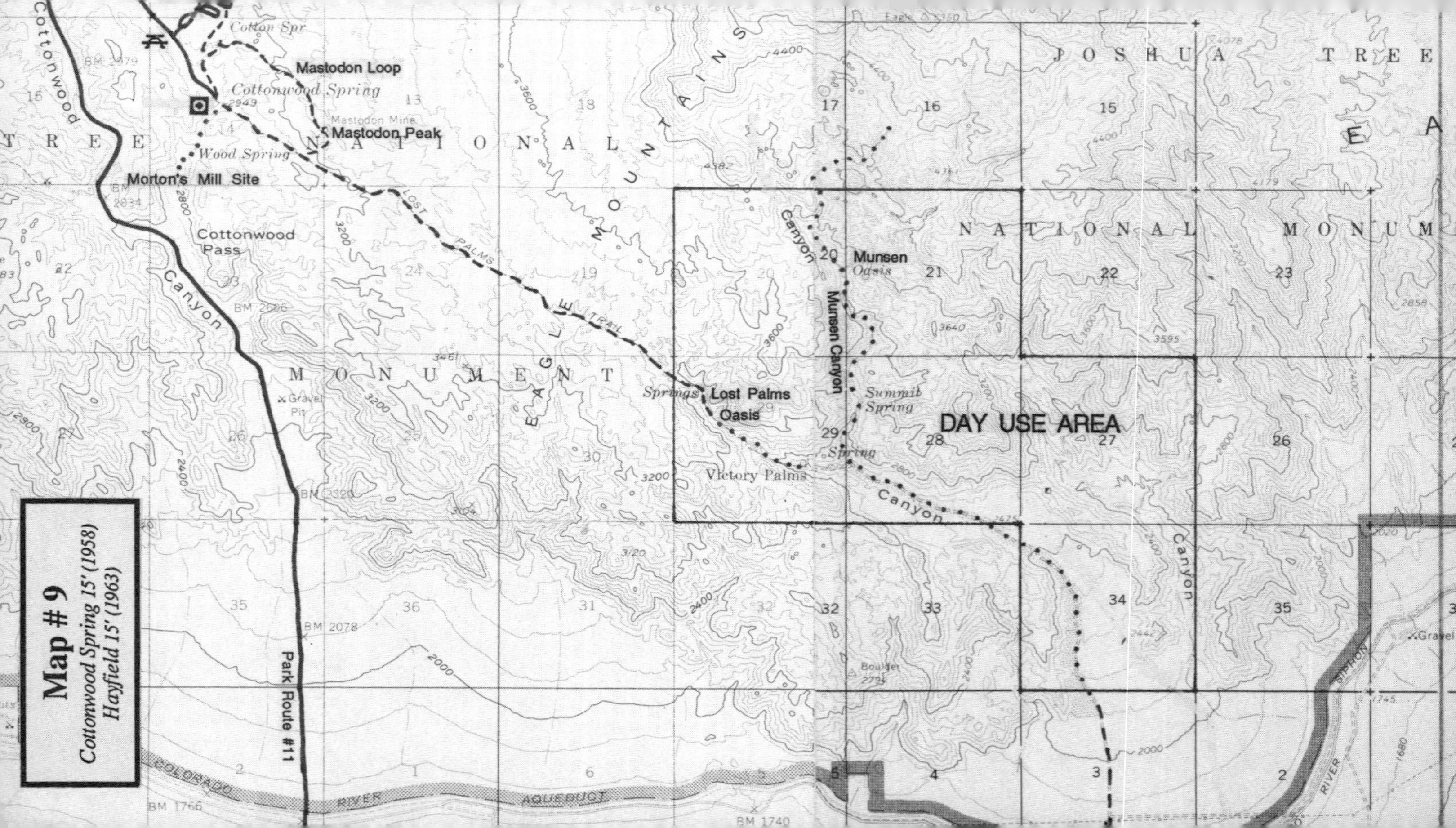
Map # 9
Cottonwood Spring 15′ (1958)
Hayfield 15′ (1963)
Cottonwood
Cotton Spr
Mastodon Loop
Cottonwood Spring
Mastodon Mine
Mastodon Peak
Wood Spring
Morton's Mill Site
Cottonwood Pass
Canyon
LOST PALMS
EAGLE TRAIL
EAGLE MOUNTAINS
JOSHUA TREE NATIONAL MONUMENT
Munsen Canyon
Munsen Oasis
Springs
Lost Palms Oasis
Summit Spring
Spring
Victory Palms
DAY USE AREA
Gravel Pit
Park Route #11
Boulder
COLORADO RIVER AQUEDUCT
RIVER SIPHON
Gravel

*Map # 10 - USGS topographical map: Cadiz Valley 15' (1956)*

# INDEX

## References and Suggested Readings

Bagley, Helen. *Sand in My Shoe.* Twentynine Palms, California: Homestead Press, 1978.

Cates, Robert. *Joshua Tree National Monument: A Visitor's Guide.*, Chatsworth, California: Live Oak Press, 1984.

Greene, Linda W. *Historic Resource Study: A History of Land Use in Joshua Tree National Monument.* Denver, Colorado: U.S. Dept. of Interior, Denver Service Center, 1983.

Jaeger, Edmund C. *The California Deserts.* Stanford, California: Stanford University Press, 1965.

James, George Wharton. *The Wonders of the Colorado Desert.* Boston, MA: Little, Brown & Co., 1907.

Joshua Tree Natural History Association. Leaflet series on flora, fauna, history, and geology of the monument.

Miller, Ronald Dean. *Mines of the High Desert.* Glendale, California: La Siesta Press, 1965.

Trails Illustrated Topo Maps. *Joshua Tree National Monument.* Evergreen, Colorado: Ponderosa Publishing Co., 1990

Trimble, Stephen. *Joshua Tree: desert reflections.* Twentynine Palms, California: Joshua Tree Natural History Association, 1979.